The basics of PEN DRAWING

Ajay

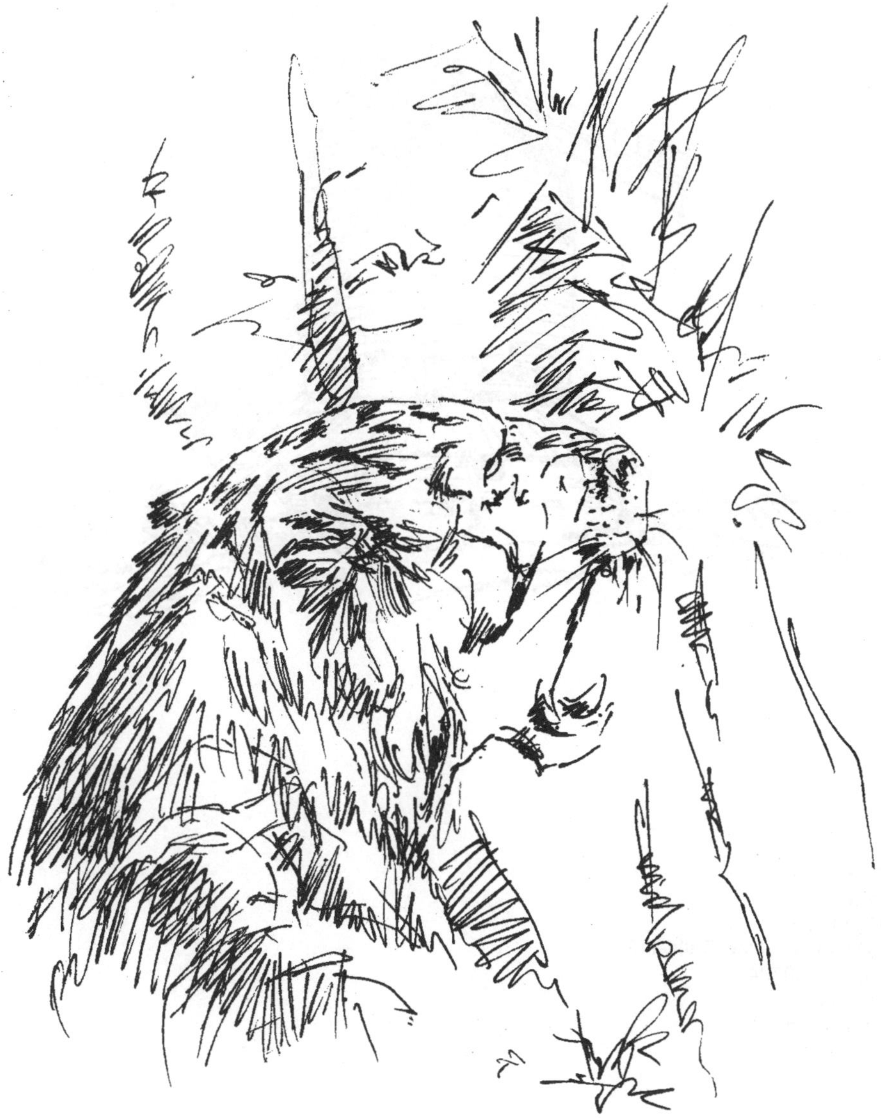

UNICORN BOOKS

Dedication

To my wife, without her it would never have been possible.

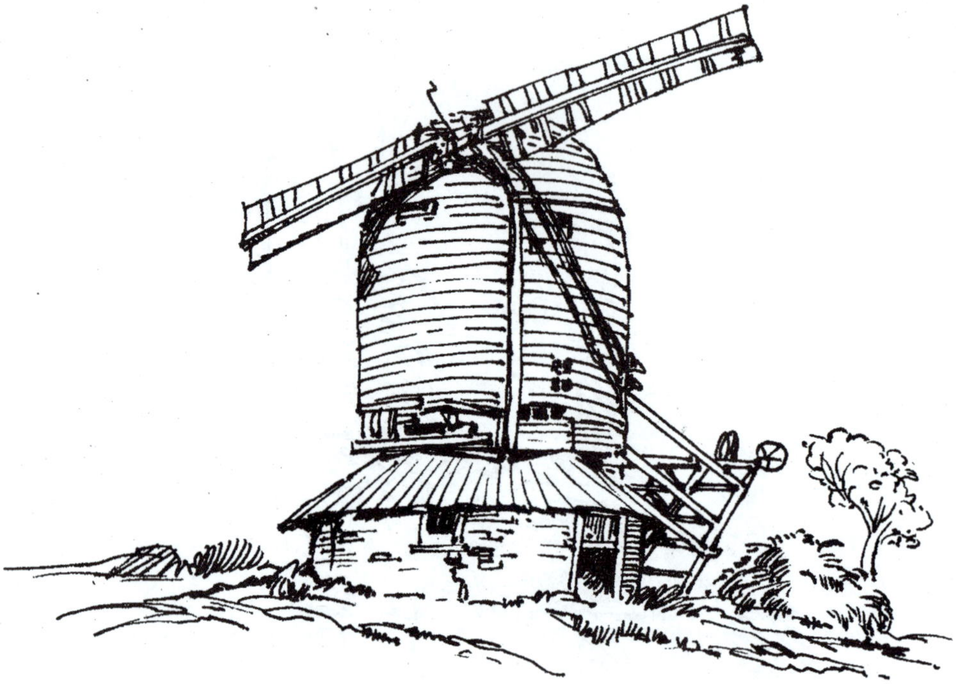

ISBN: 978-81-7806-135-1
The Basics of Pen Drawing
UNICORN BOOKS (P) Ltd.
F-2/16, Ansari Road, Daryaganj, New Delhi-110002
Phones: 011-23262683, 23250704
E-mail: info@unicornbooks.in
Website: www.unicornbooks.in

Contents

Introduction

Pen—The Wonder Tool

How many times have you used that pen of yours? Start counting and you will realise that it is not possible to remember. Every day of your past life you had been using it. Have you ever thought about using it as a drawing tool? This good old pen (it may be ball or gel) of yours can produce really excellent drawings.

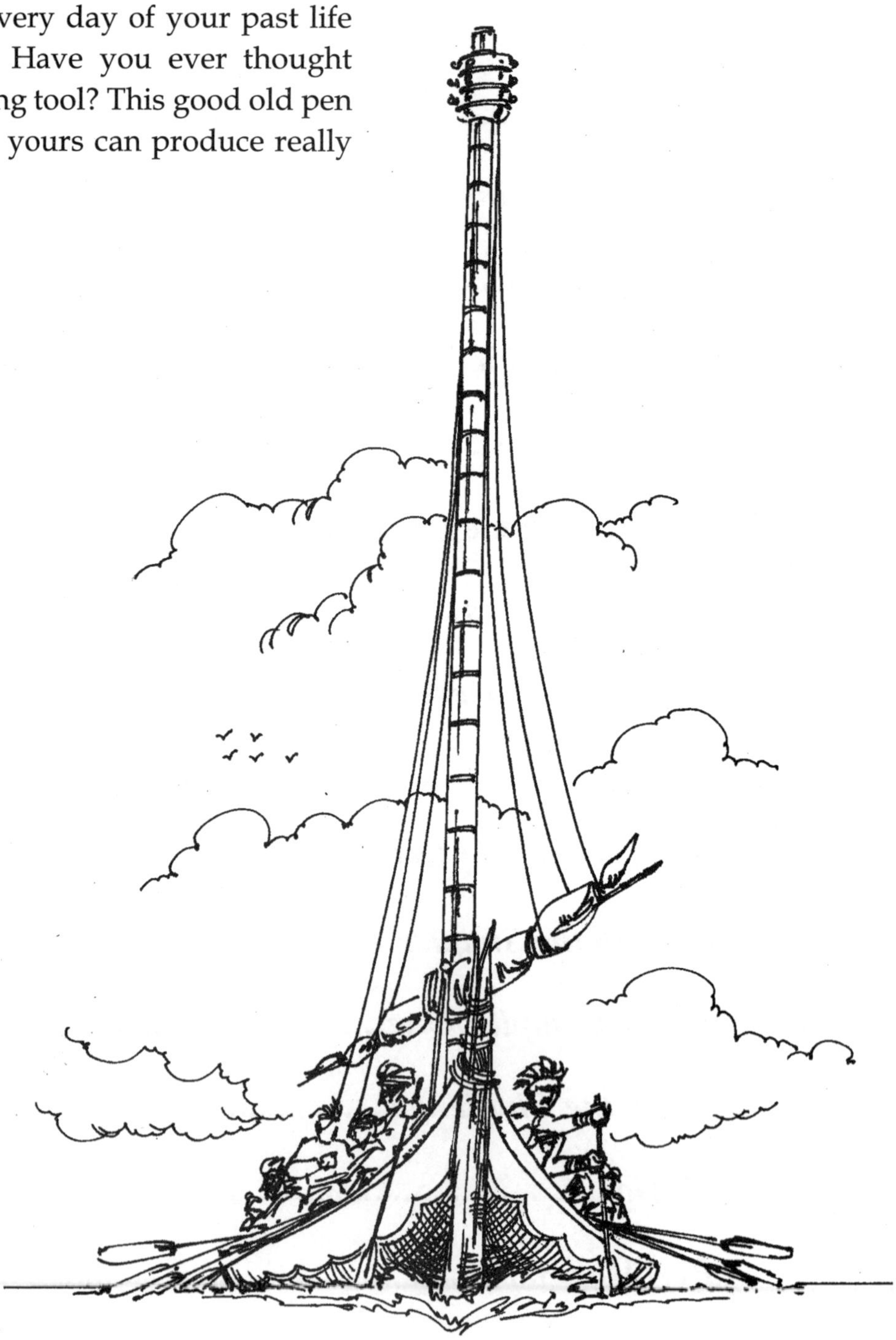

Keep some basic thumb rules in mind and you will be on your way. First use pencil to block the drawing of the subject. Then use pen (black ball or gel pens are good) to draw the sketch within blocked area. In pen drawing, everything is created by using lines in various ways. Always keep the shape of the object you are drawing in your mind. Your lines should follow its stops and curvatures. The pressure on the pen tip and grip of hand should be very light. Move your whole hand from elbow to fingers when drawing big shapes. It will give you more freedom and confidence. So, shall we start?

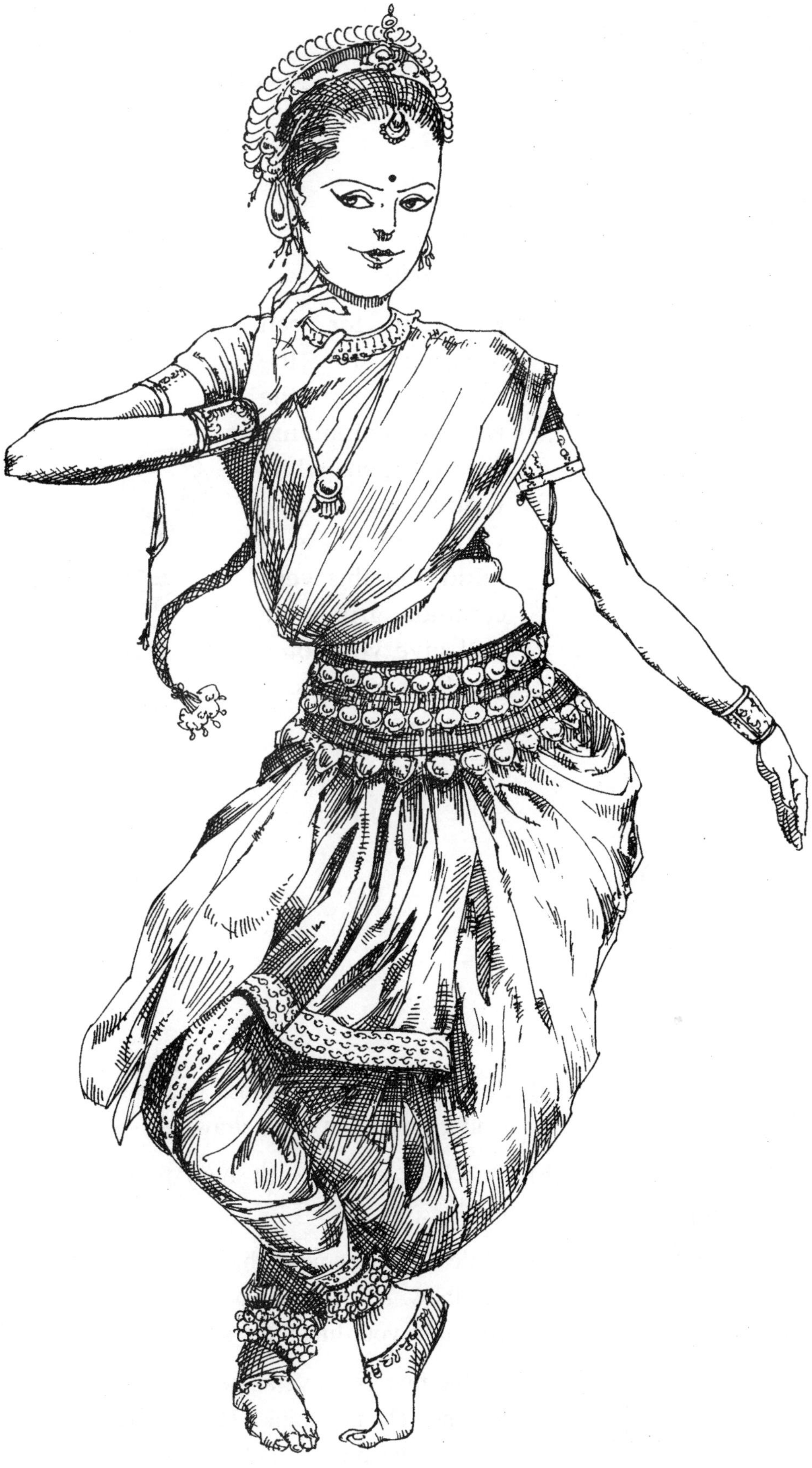

Some Basic Things

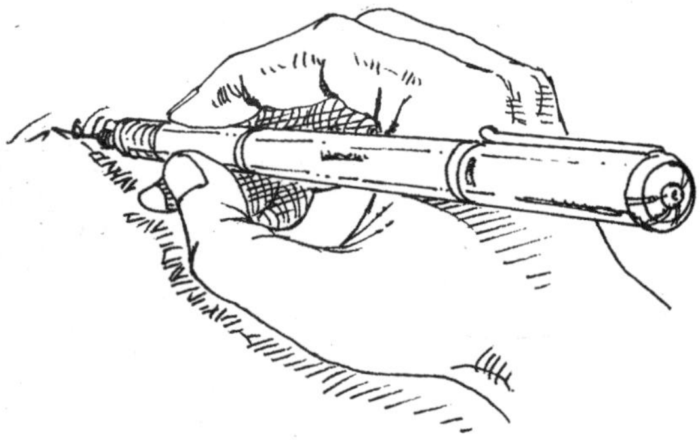

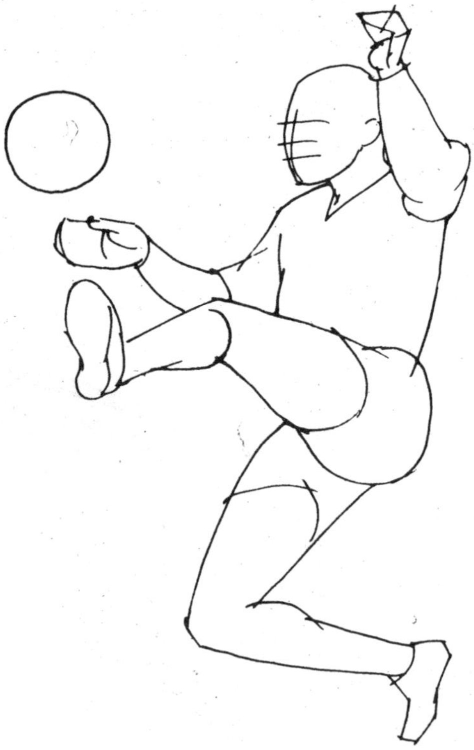

The Grip

Handgrip for pen drawing is the natural one, the way we commonly hold our pens while writing. Keep some very simple things in mind and this very common grip style will give you some excellent pictures.

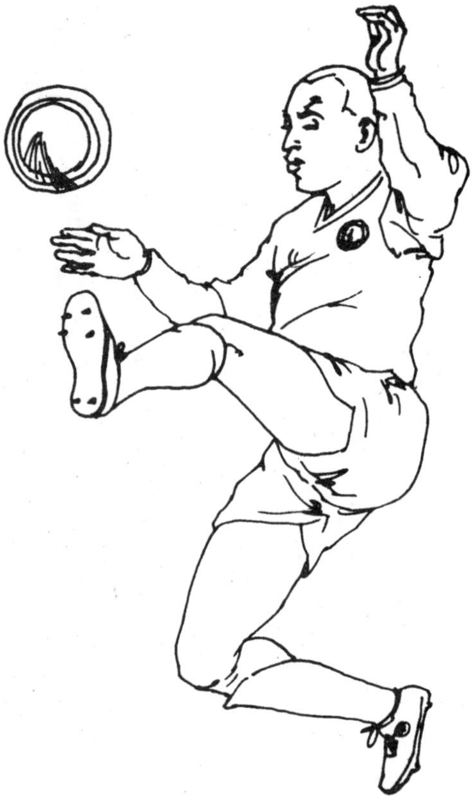

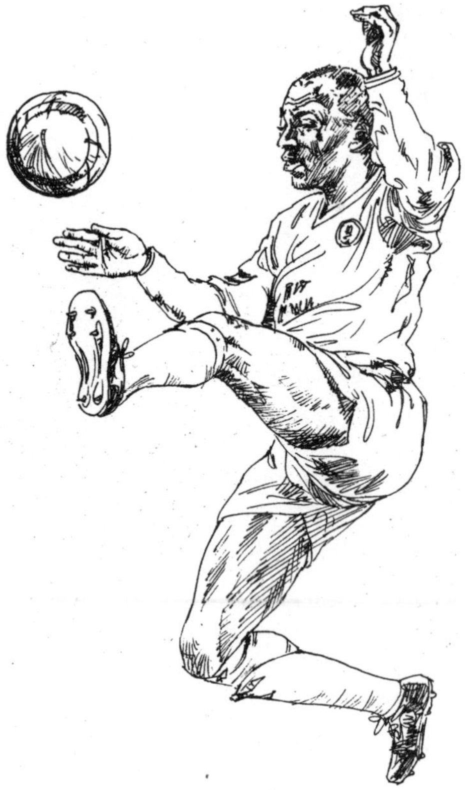

(a) Do not hold the pen close to the tip. It will obstruct your hand's movement while drawing.

(b) Grab it at least an inch away from the pen tip and hold it lightly.

(c) While drawing, move the whole hand—from the fingers to the elbow. It will give you extra manoeuvring capacity, and will make your line more smooth.

(d) Let the fingers move as per the lines of the picture you are drawing. Do not think. There should not be any thoughts between the picture and your fingers. Eyes should see the picture and hand should draw it.

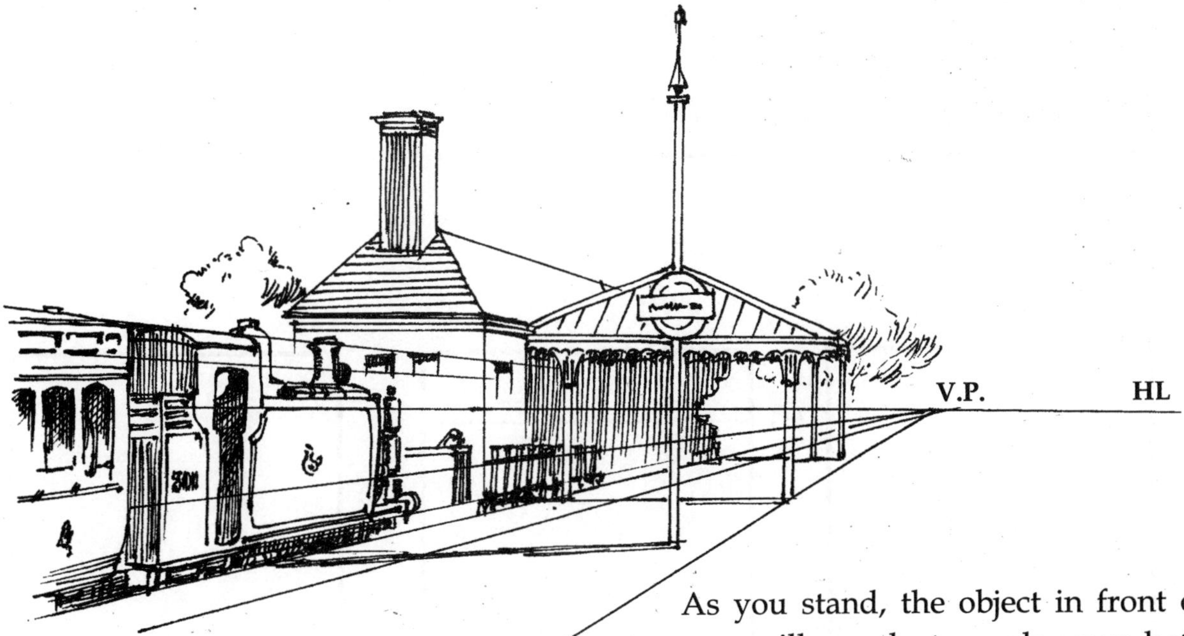

As you stand, the object in front of you will recede towards your both sides, and if go on, will vanish at some point on horizon line.

The Perspective

Two of the most important and fundamental rules of seeing things are as follows:

(a) Objects get reduced in size as they recede towards the vanishing point (where things seem to get mixed and lose their shapes), which is situated on the horizon line.

(b) The object placed in front of another will hide those parts that fall behind the first one.

Natural proportion of an object, the angle and area of view, and the perspective rules when mingled together can produce an excellent drawing.

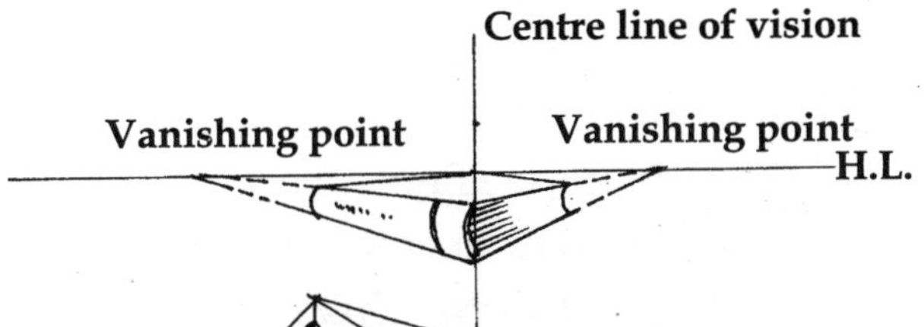

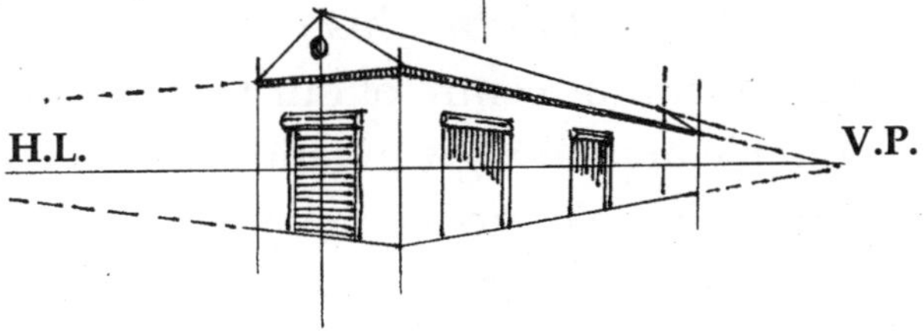

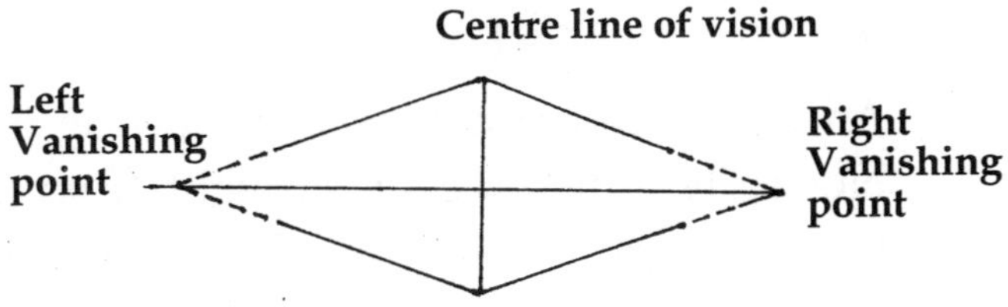

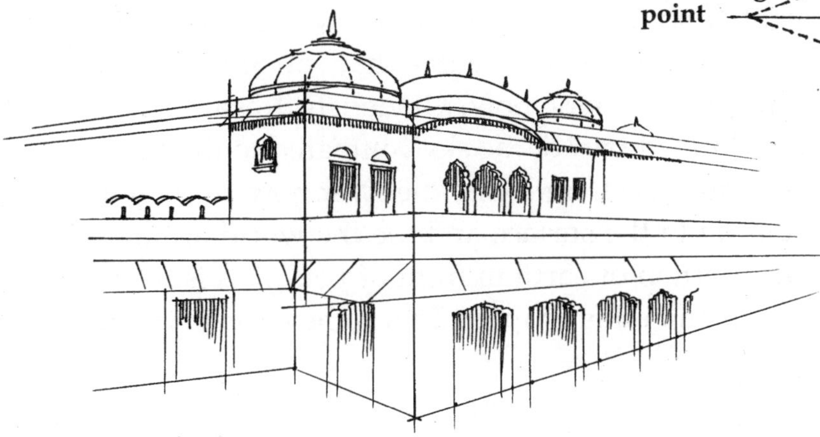

Centre line of vision

Things recede and become more pointed as they go towards horizon line.

The View and Viewfinder

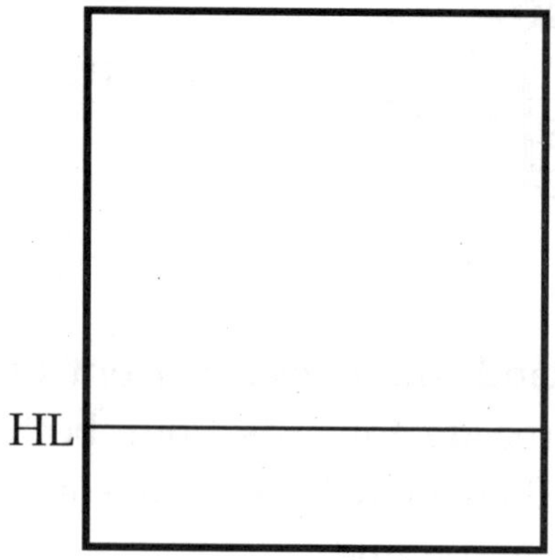

Standard view

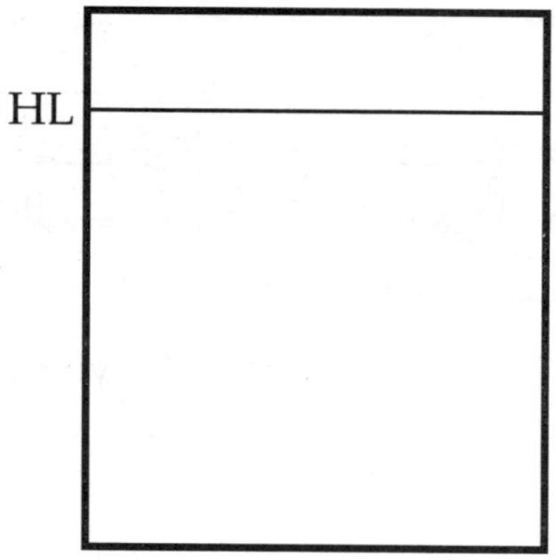

Bird view

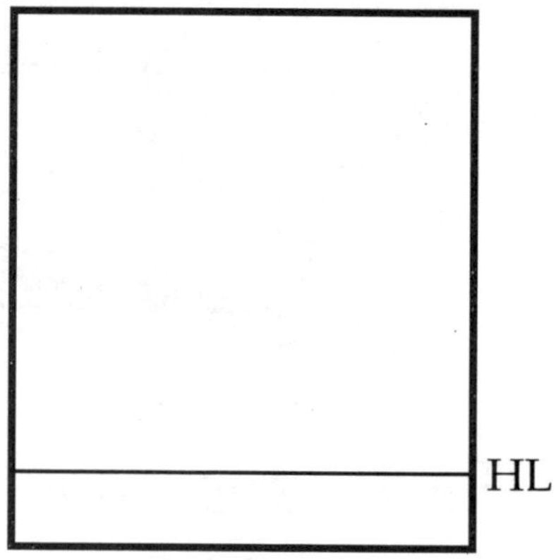

Frog view

Have you ever noticed that when you are seeing straight, the vision of the side areas of the landscape is not clear. But when you move your head to one side, the things of this part will become clear and the objects of the previous direction will turn into a blurred form. This happens because our viewing capacity is limited on both sides from the centre of our focal point. Due to this limitation, we have to choose a suitable area in a given landscape or composition to produce a more focussed and impressive picture. Here comes the role of viewfinder. It is a rectangular piece of frame of cardboard or thick paper that allows the viewer to see and select a certain part of a picture more effectively. You can move it all over the picture until you find the most suitable part to draw.

Another important aspect of viewing is the position of horizon line in a picture. Normally, when we see straight from a standing position, we can see more sky than the earth. This is called normal view. Now imagine that you are a bird, flying gracefully in the sky. Where will you be looking now? Obviously, towards the earth. And this time you can see a very limited part of the sky compared to the earth. It is bird view. Drop from the heaven and go straight into the river now. Well, you will need air to breathe. So come out on to the surface and see the world around. You will see the vast sky and a small portion of earth in front of you. This is frog view. See all these examples carefully given in this chapter. This is the basic placement of a drawing.

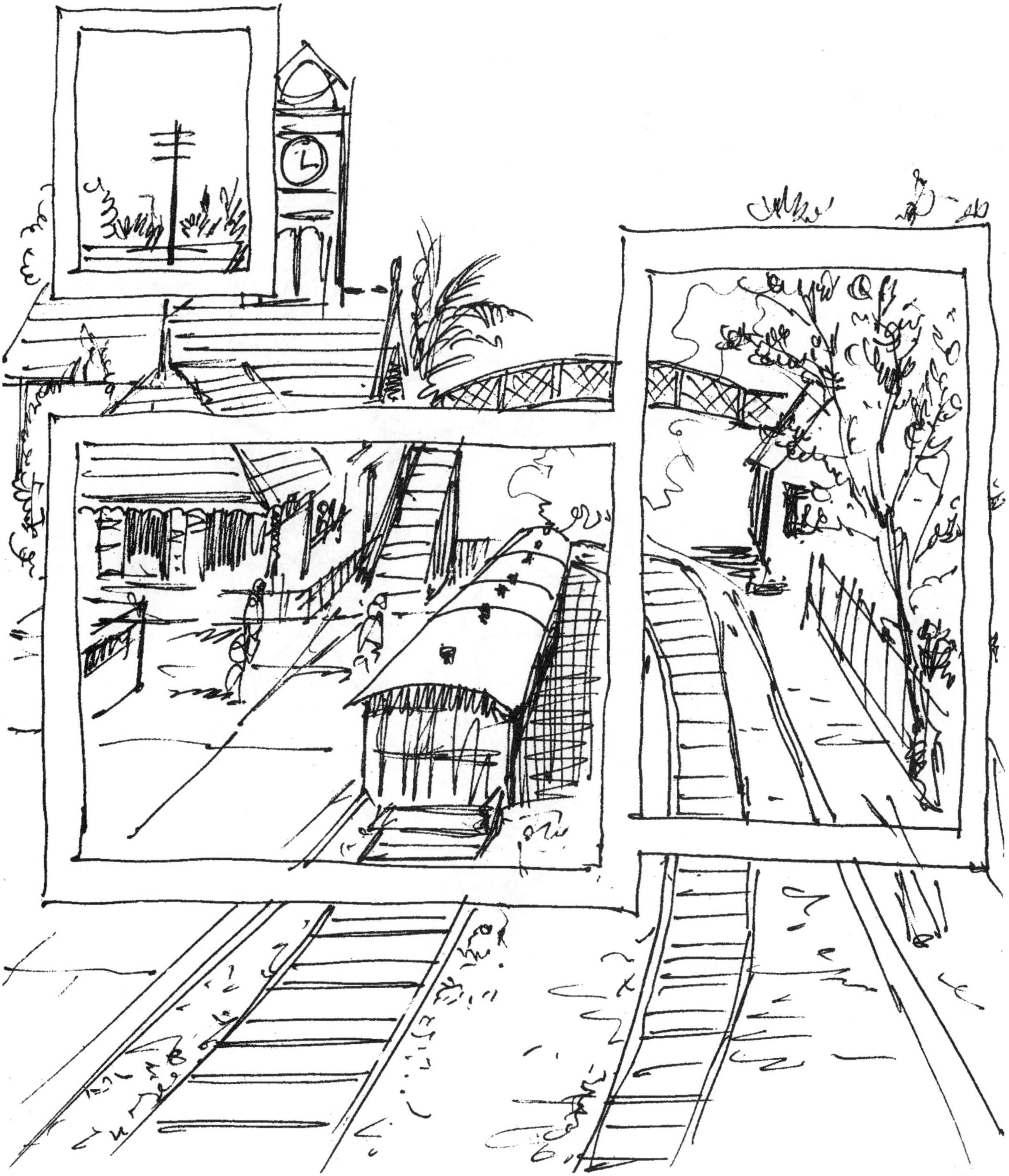

Lines & Strokes

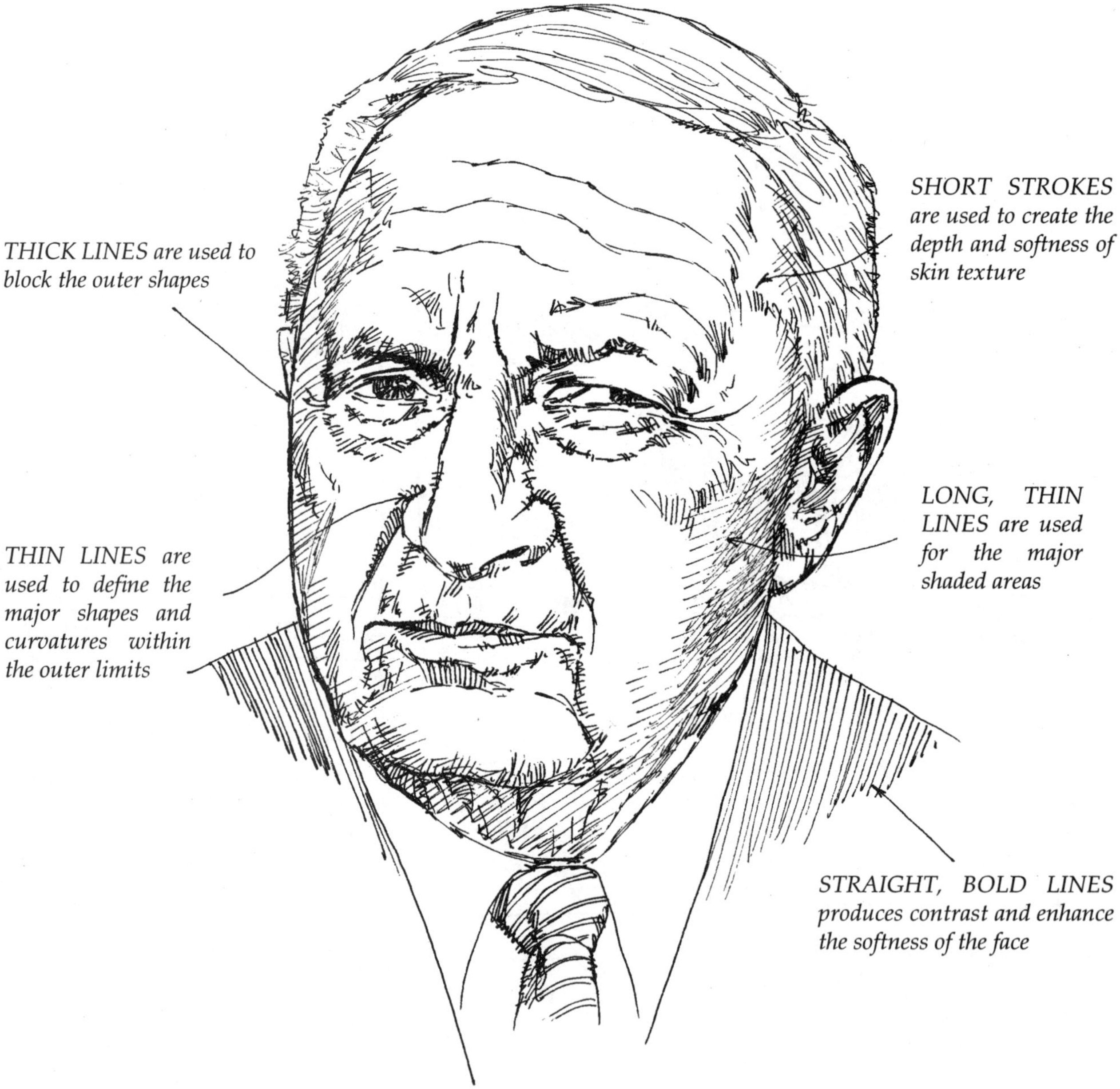

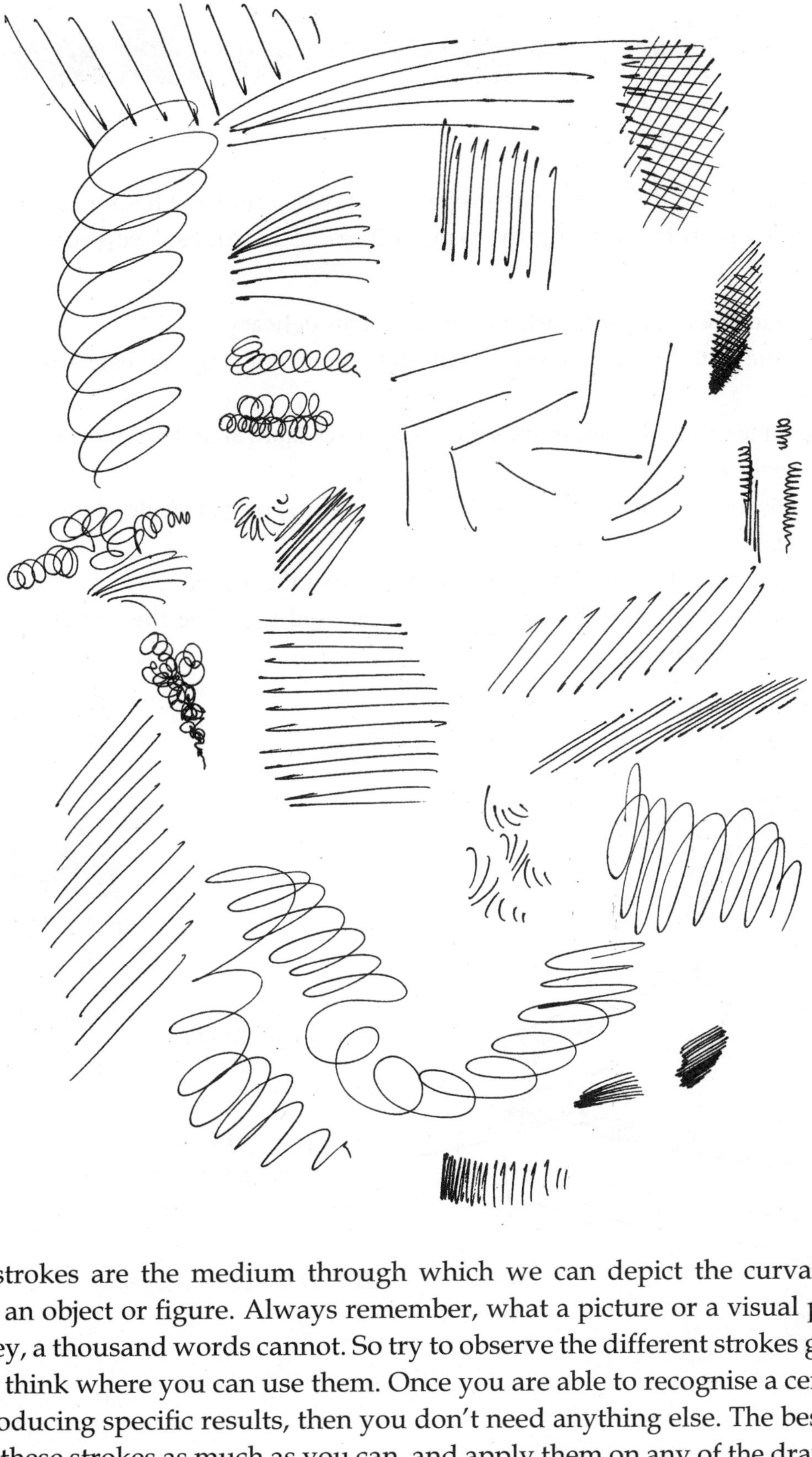

Various strokes are the medium through which we can depict the curvatures of the planes of an object or figure. Always remember, what a picture or a visual presentation can convey, a thousand words cannot. So try to observe the different strokes given on this page and think where you can use them. Once you are able to recognise a certain type of stroke producing specific results, then you don't need anything else. The best way to do it is copy these strokes as much as you can, and apply them on any of the drawings given in this book.

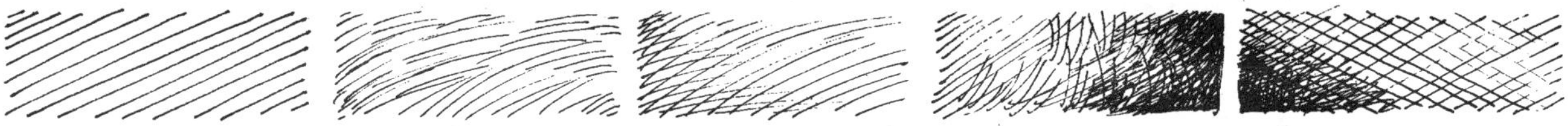

Once we have decided what our subject to draw is and how it should look like, then we move on to choosing the type of lines and strokes. Keep some simple tips in mind.

a) Thin line produces a soft surface and represents delicacy.
b) Thin line with graded thickness will make your drawing graduate from soft to hard.
c) Thick line creates hardness and appears to cover more area. Heaviness can also be achieved by these lines.
d) By reducing or increasing the gap between strokes, you can create more softness or hardness.
e) Length of a stroke is useful in defining the size of the object.
f) Direction and the length of a stroke can be used to define the curvature of the surface of an object.

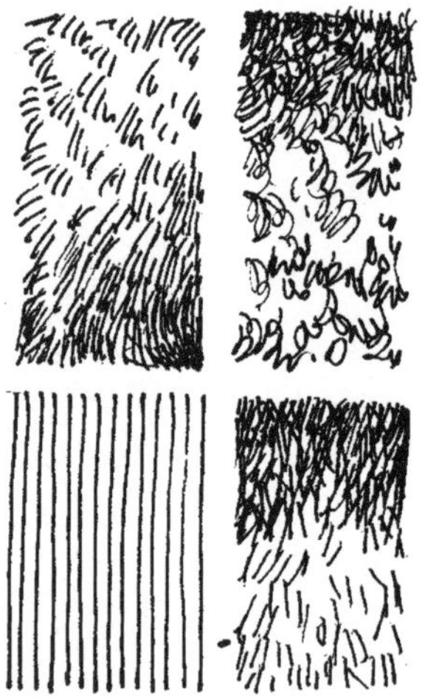

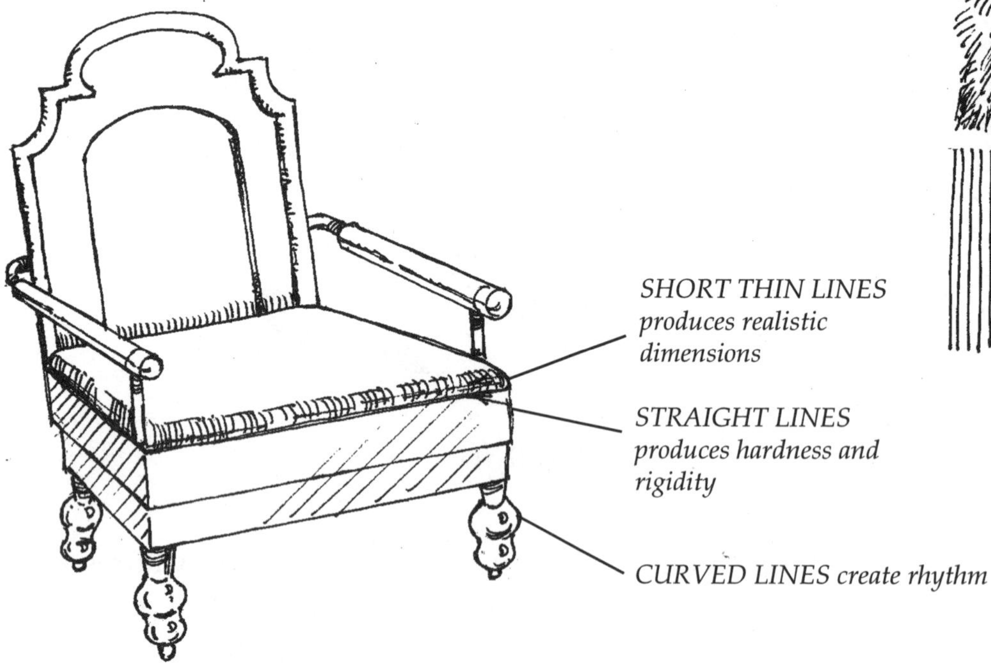

The Light, Shade and Shadows

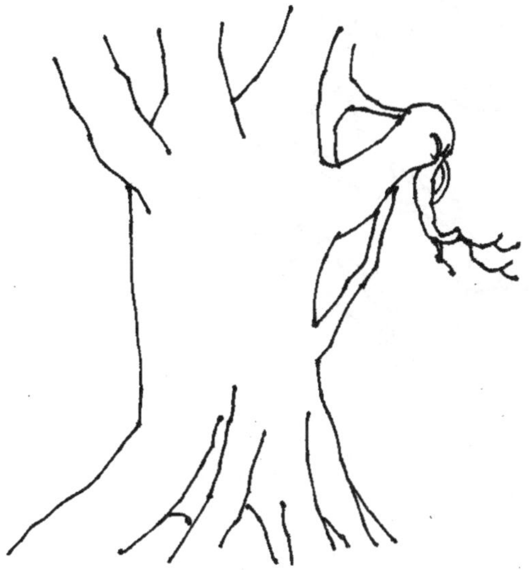

Outline

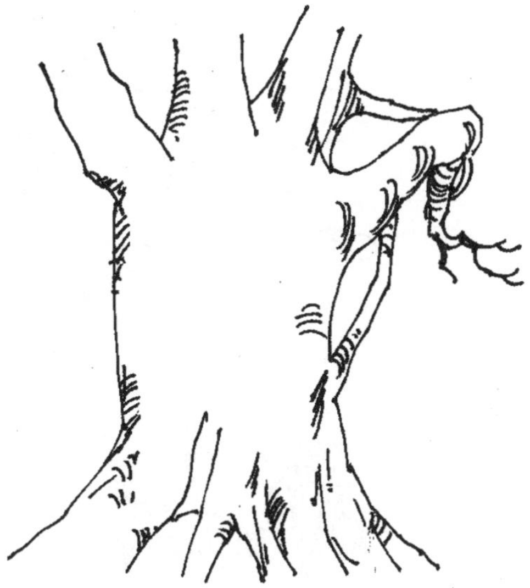

Form

All the objects in their natural existence have got three dimensions while our paper is only of two. As a picture or composition is a representation of its natural form, we have to create this third dimension to add some credibility to our line drawing. Only the light falling on an object can make it possible. See the example of trees given here and you will get a feel of what we mean.

Light source is the main factor in this arrangement and the individual shape of the object is the other one. When light falls on an object, it creates volume and defines planes of curvature as per its individual shape. As the light goes further away from its source, it creates different tones.

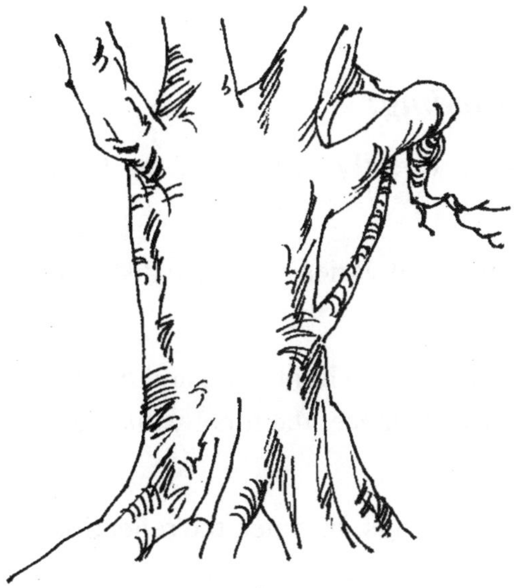

Accent

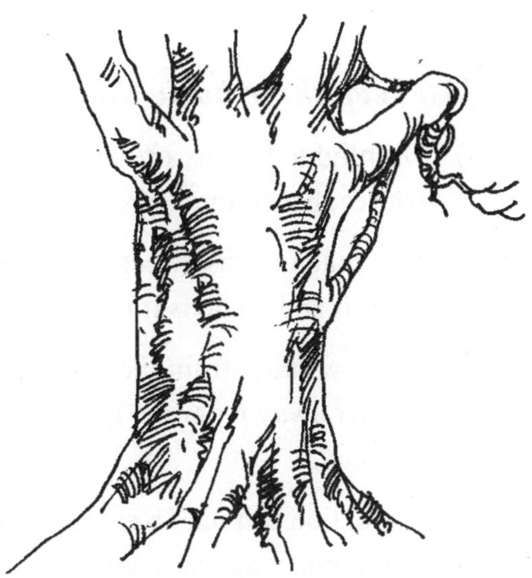

Texture

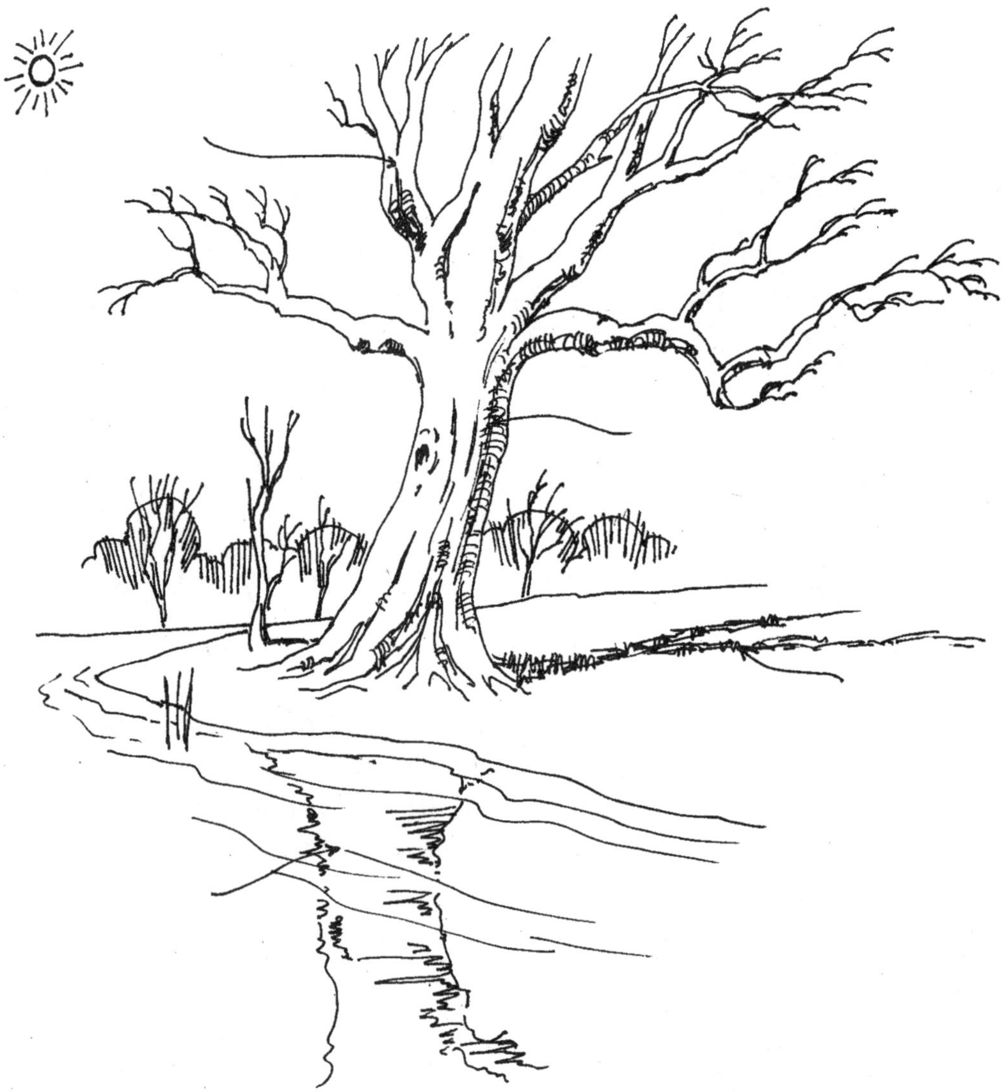

Just keep these basic things in mind when shading:

a) Highlighted areas on an object are those that fall directly in front of the light source, hence the nearest two.

b) The shade forms directly opposite of the light source but varies as per the distance from it and so does it tones.

c) Shadow starts from the base of the object where there is no light at all and moves further away from the light source. As it covers the distance, the tonal value gets reduced.

d) Reflection can only be seen in the water or glasslike things. In water, the reflection of an object appears directly below and in glass, right in front.

The Basic Shapes

This is the last thing you have to learn before drawing anything. Basic shapes are the simplified forms of complex natural things. Once you get familiar with these forms and become expert in drawing, you will automatically become casual in approach. Same thing happens with the complex drawings and compositions (with the passing of time). Carefully observe the individual shape of an object given here and the source of light. When mingled together they produce subtle grades of tone, which in turn define surface curvature and texture. We recommend that you should copy these basic shapes as much as you can. Keep changing the source of light and note the difference. If you want to experiment further, get wooden models of these shapes. Buy a table lamp (of bulb type, not the tube) and by changing its position, you can see the light effect visually on the wooden models.

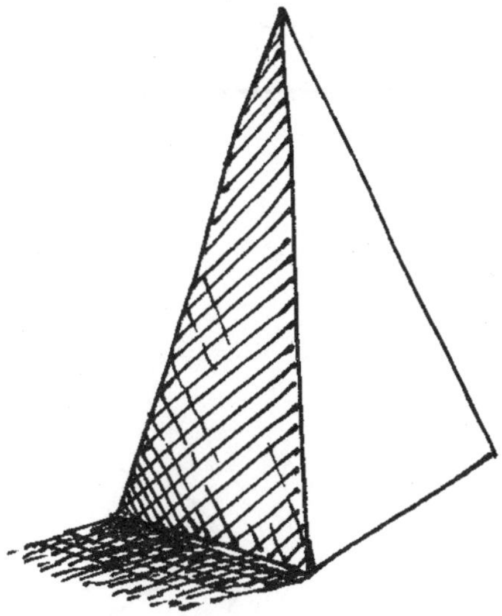

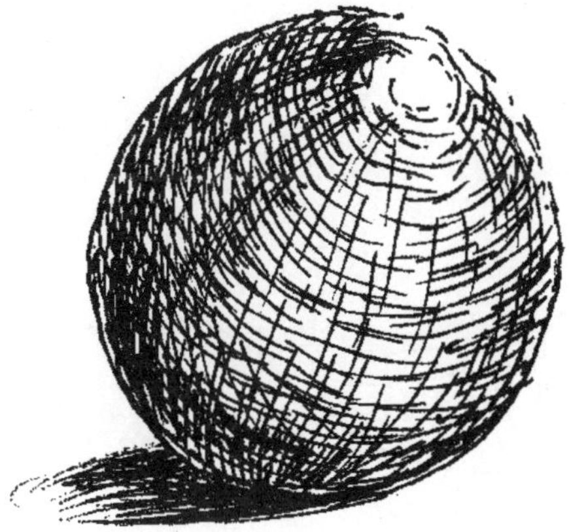

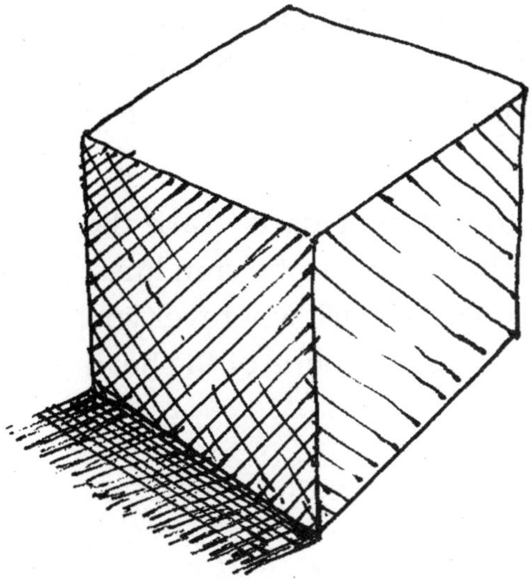

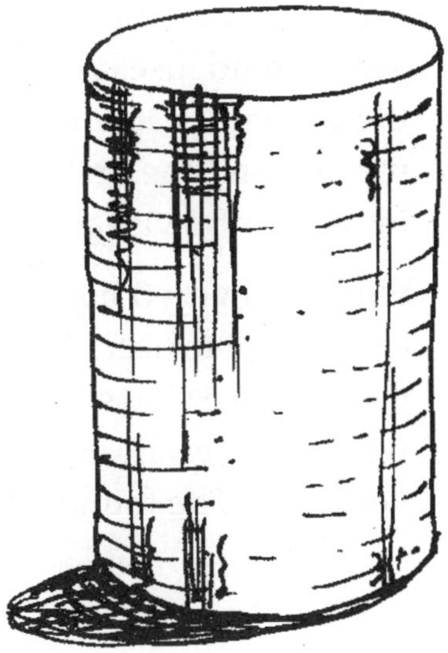

How to Start & Develop a Line Drawing

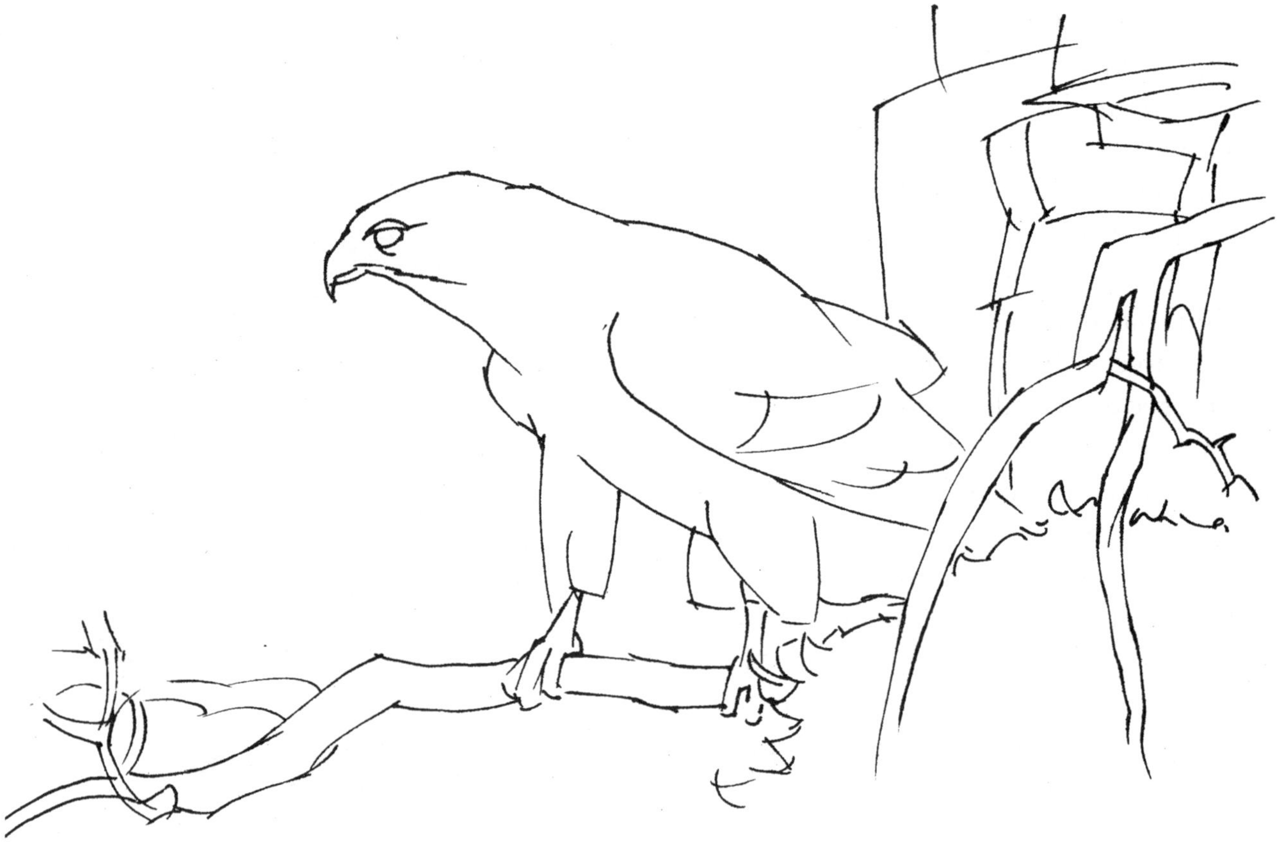

There are two types of possible approaches to start a drawing. First, you should use a pencil for basic guidelines and blockings and the second is to prepare a mental sketch of the foundations. We recommend the first approach in the beginning until you get perfect in the mental visualisation.

Simplify everything and then divide it in different parts. Take the example of a face. Instead of drawing forehead, jaw or the chin lines, use a simple oval shape for the whole head. Now mark wherever you want the eyes, nose, mouth, etc. Also place the centreline of the head vertically. The foundation is done.

Carefully note the major lines and curvatures now, and on the foundation line start placing them one by one but with more accuracy this time.

Always begin with the outlines or the lines that should block the picture. Then the other ones next. As you complete the sketch, your picture should be identifiable with the original object or photo.

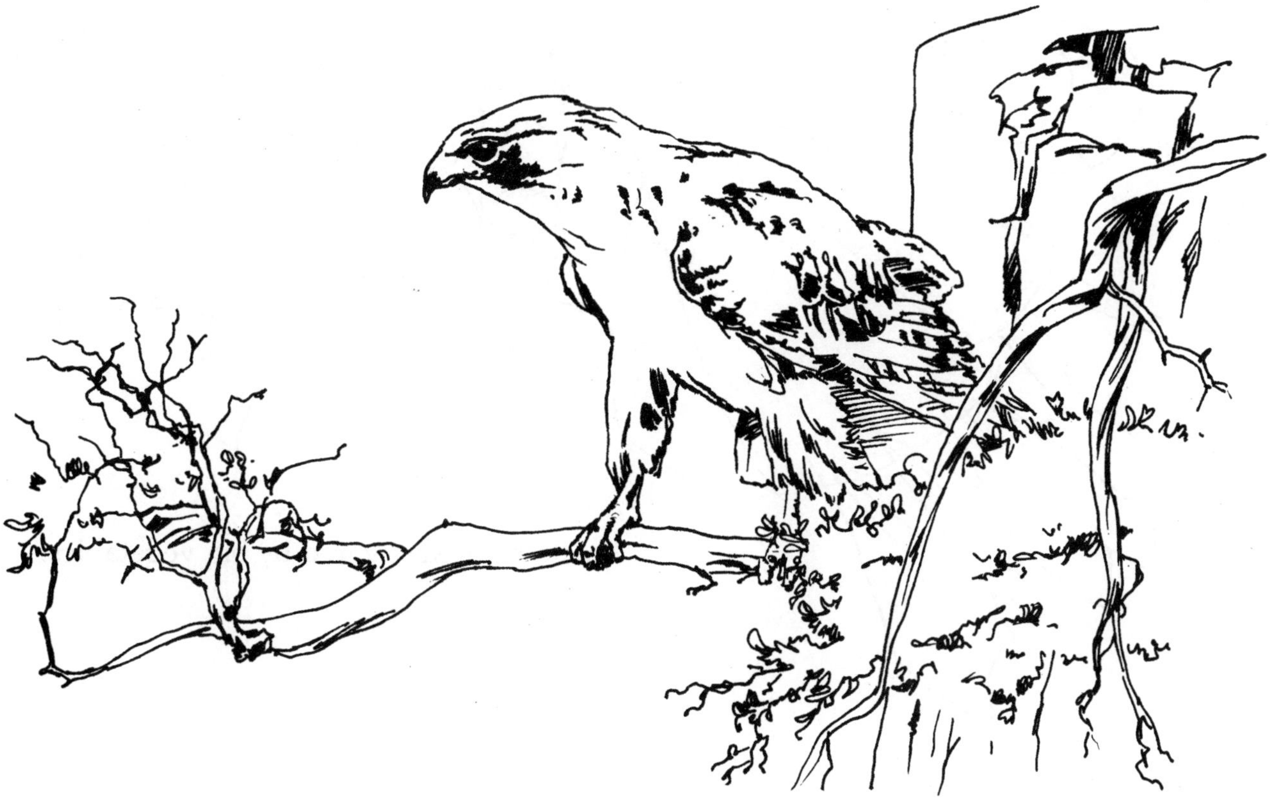

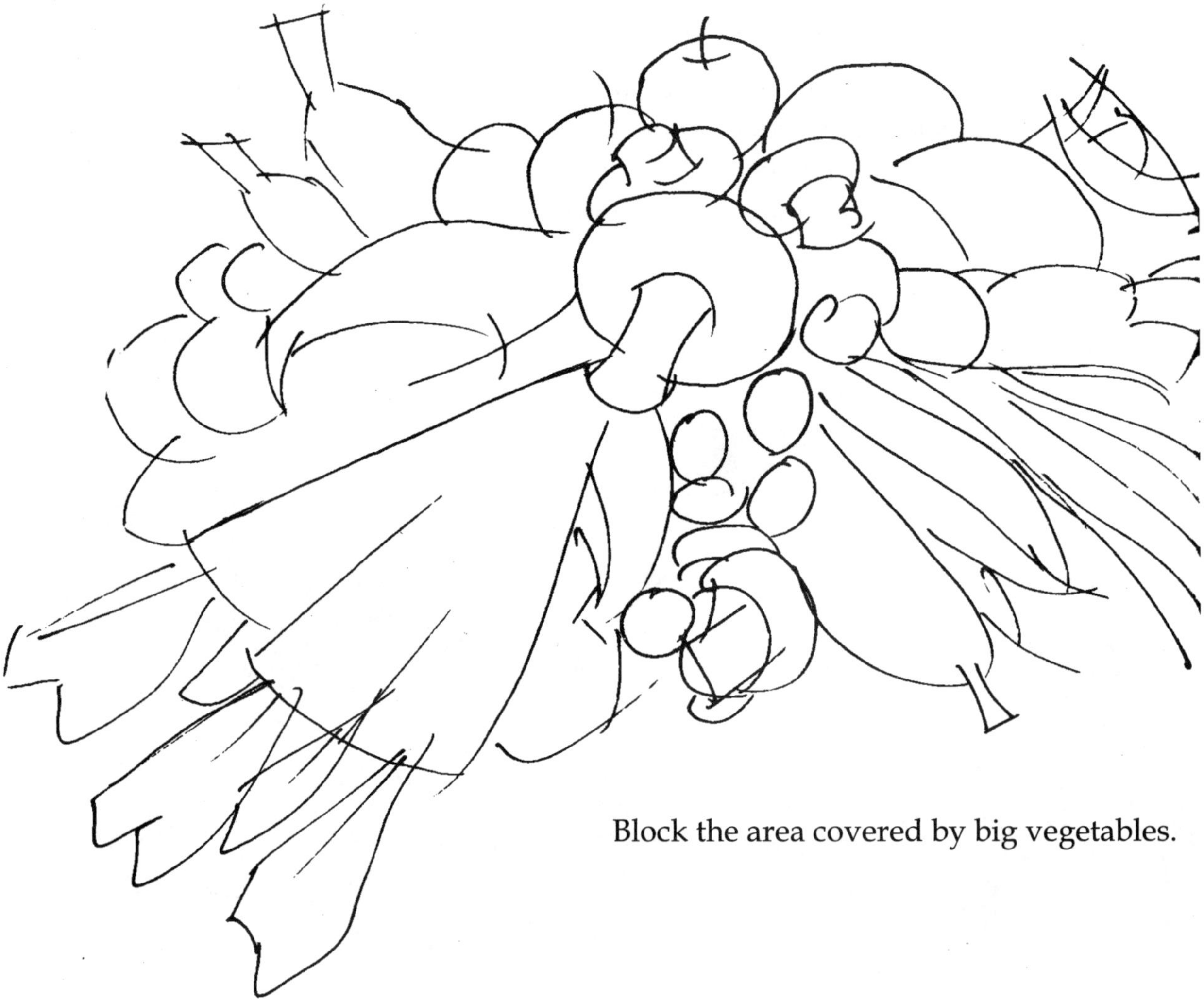

Block the area covered by big vegetables.

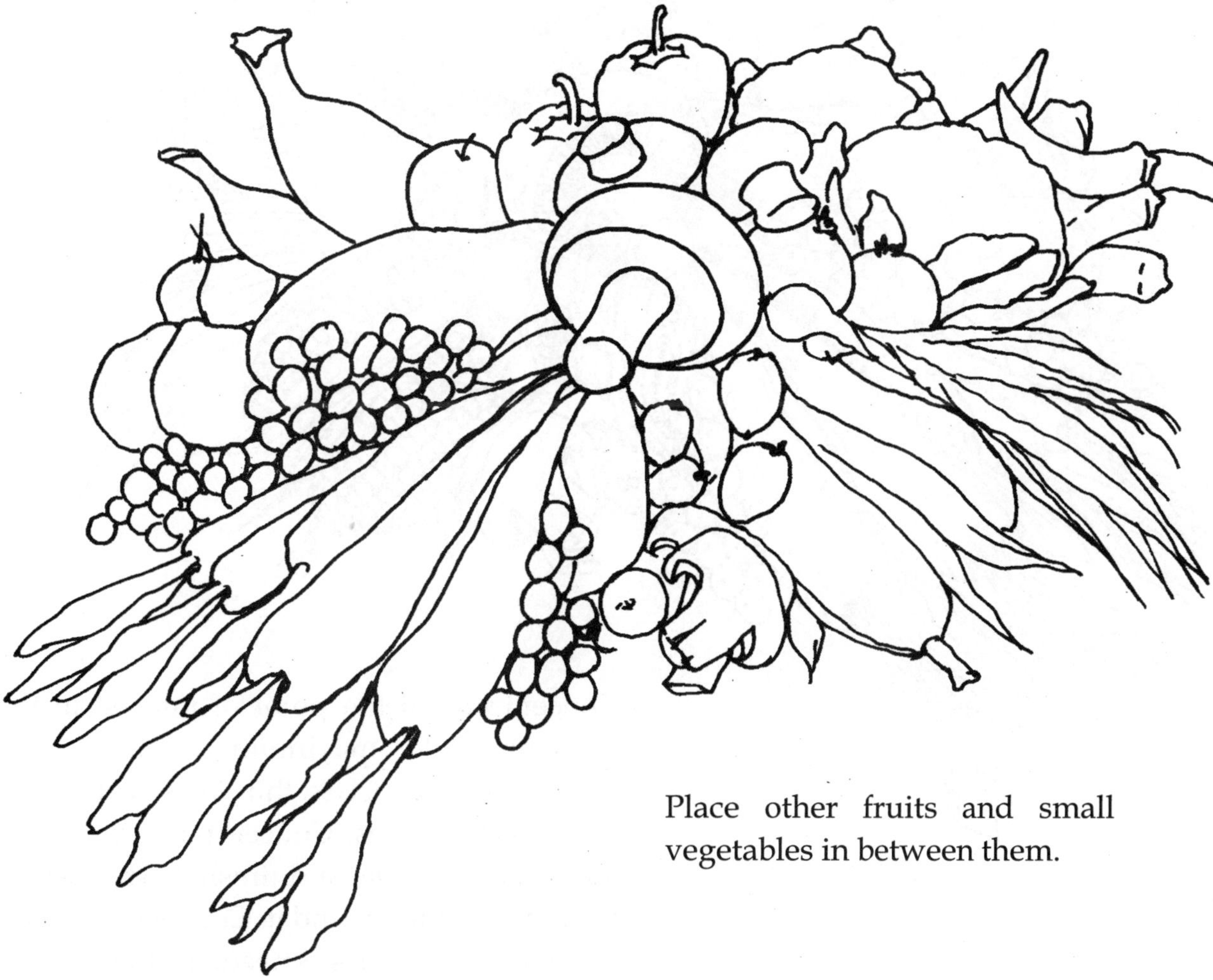

Place other fruits and small vegetables in between them.

How to Finish

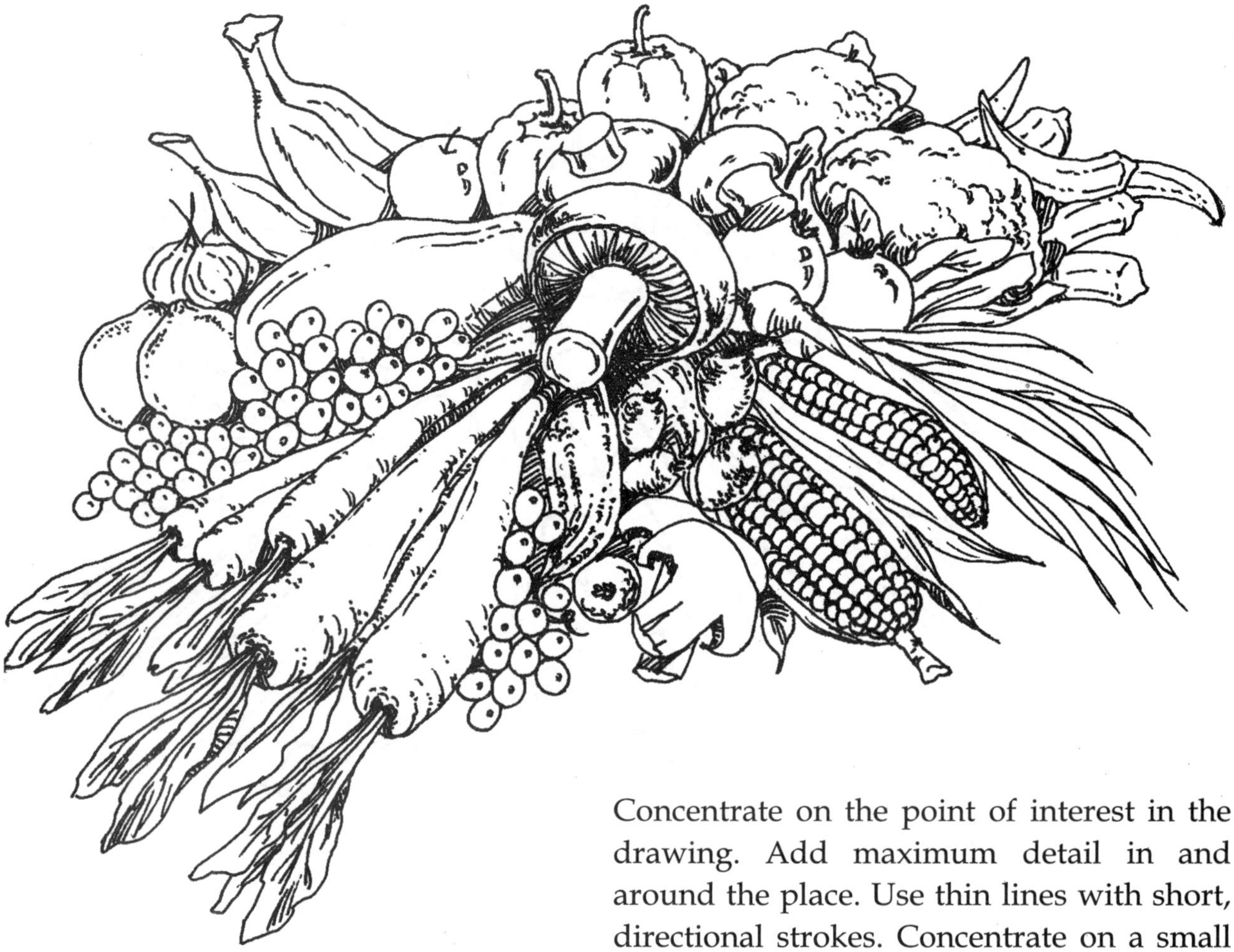

Concentrate on the point of interest in the drawing. Add maximum detail in and around the place. Use thin lines with short, directional strokes. Concentrate on a small area, one at a time, and finish it. Then finish the parts falling around it. Connect these two by short or long lines as needed. Slowly build up the whole focal point like this. As you depart from this point, reduce the details. In the end, see the finished drawing from some distance, so you can grasp it as a whole. You can add some lines here and there if you like to, otherwise it is complete now.

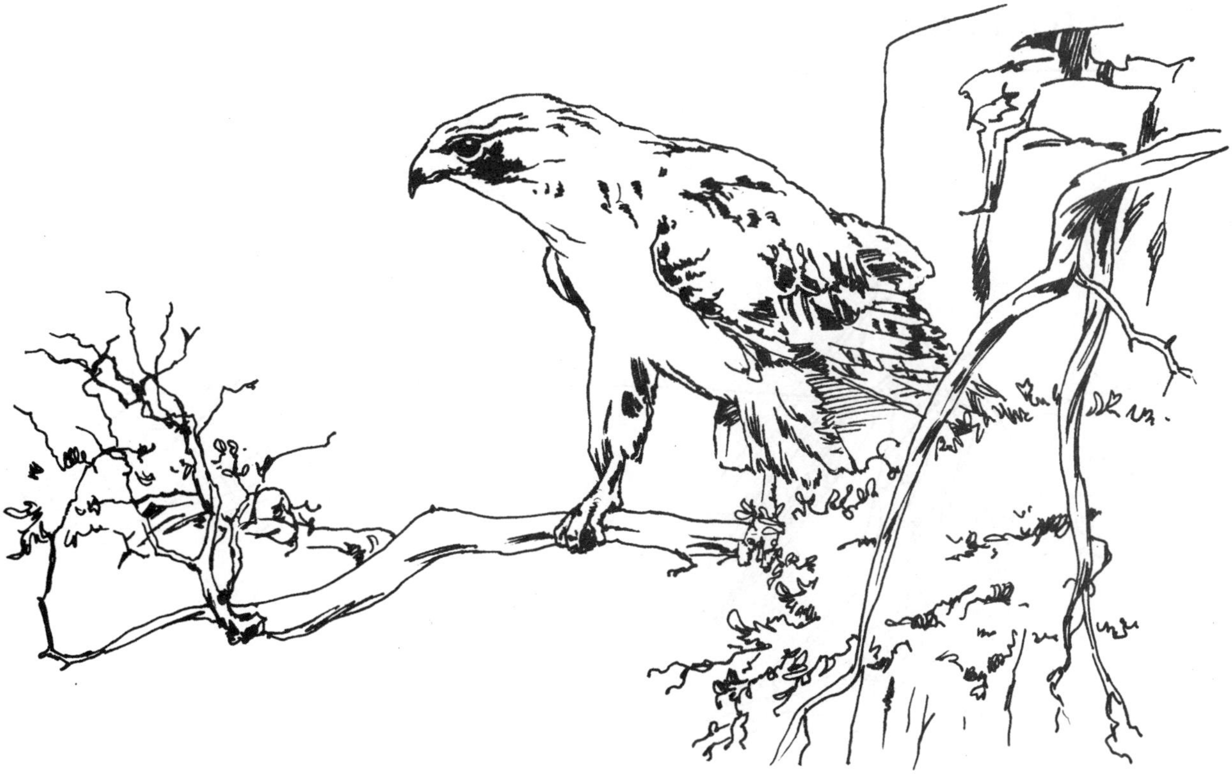

A bird of prey. It has the killing look. Cross position of the branch against the vertical lines of mountain gives the feeling of heights.

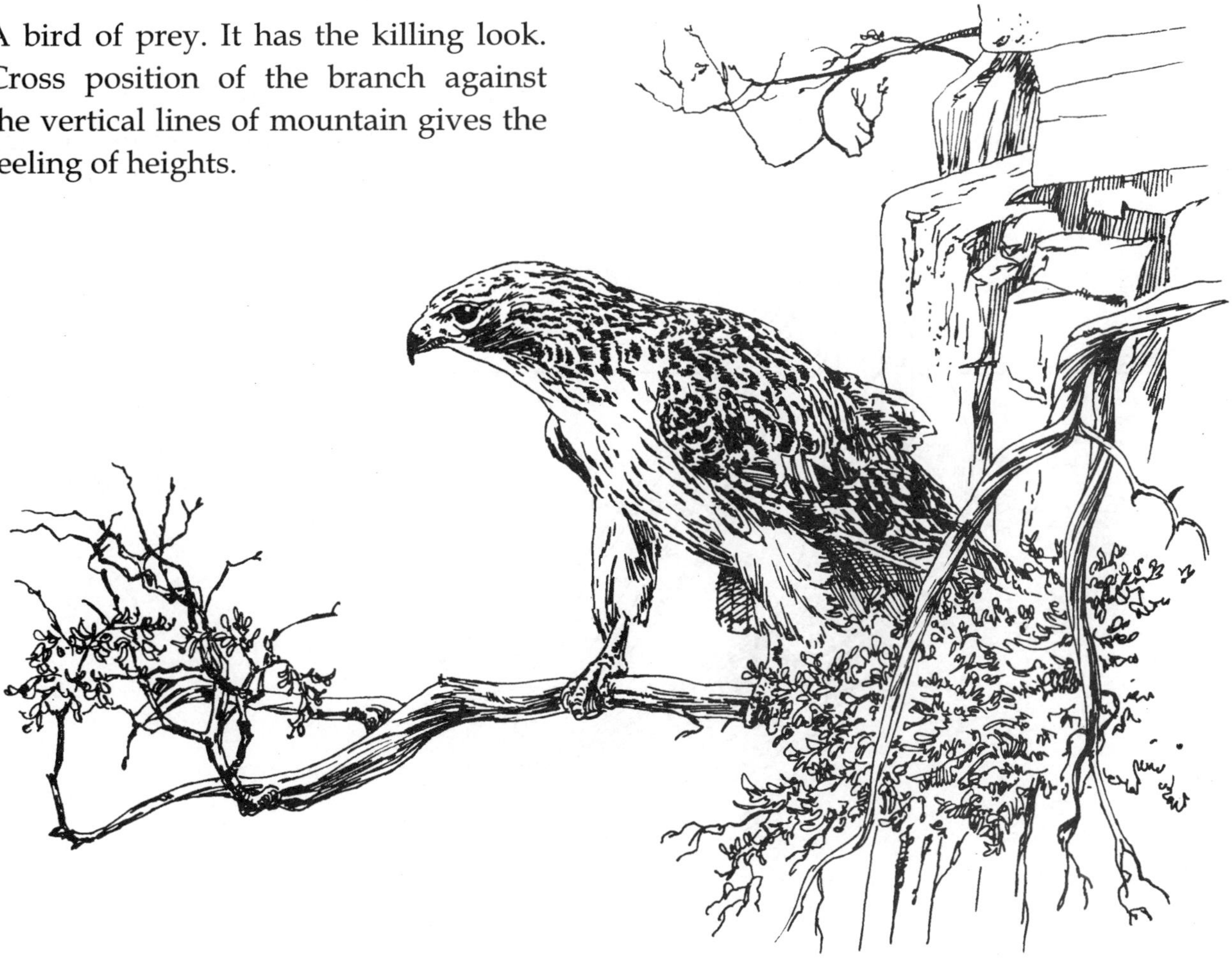

The Percentage of Details

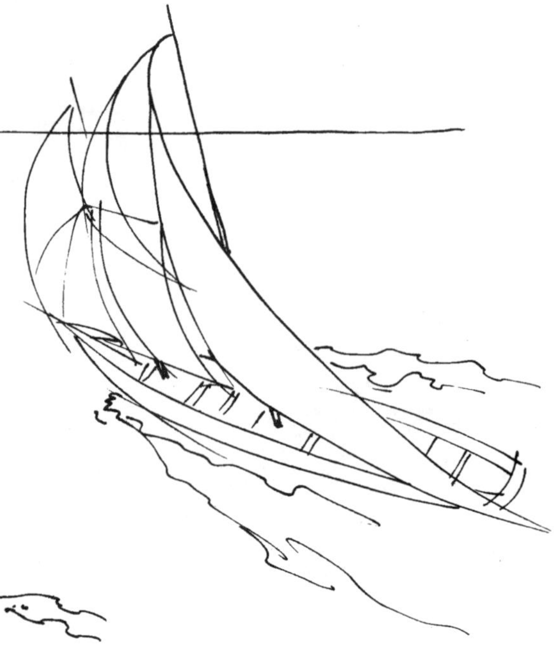

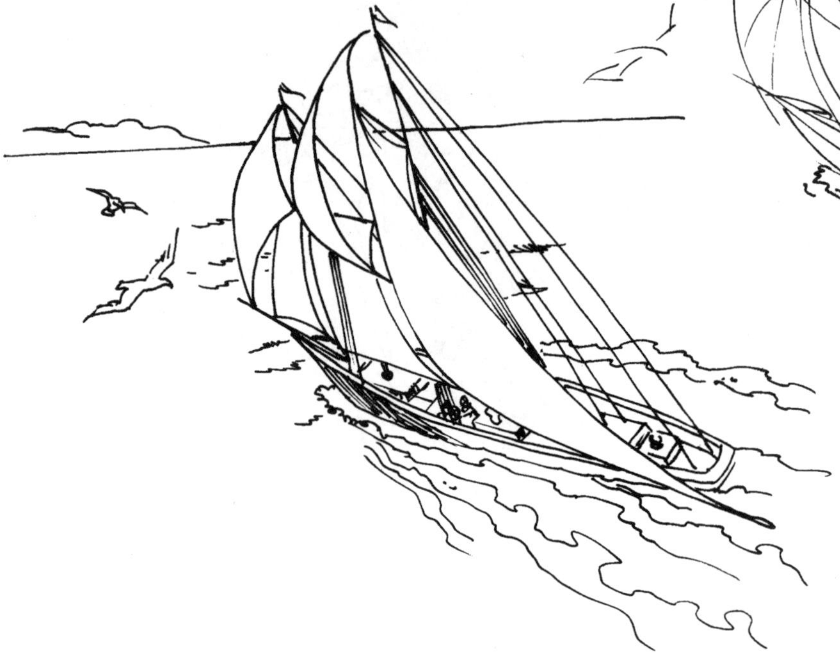

Predecided focal point is the centre around which the details should be added. Leave the other areas with less or no details at all, as per their importance. If you try to draw everything in detail as beginners generally do, the whole composition will appear flat.

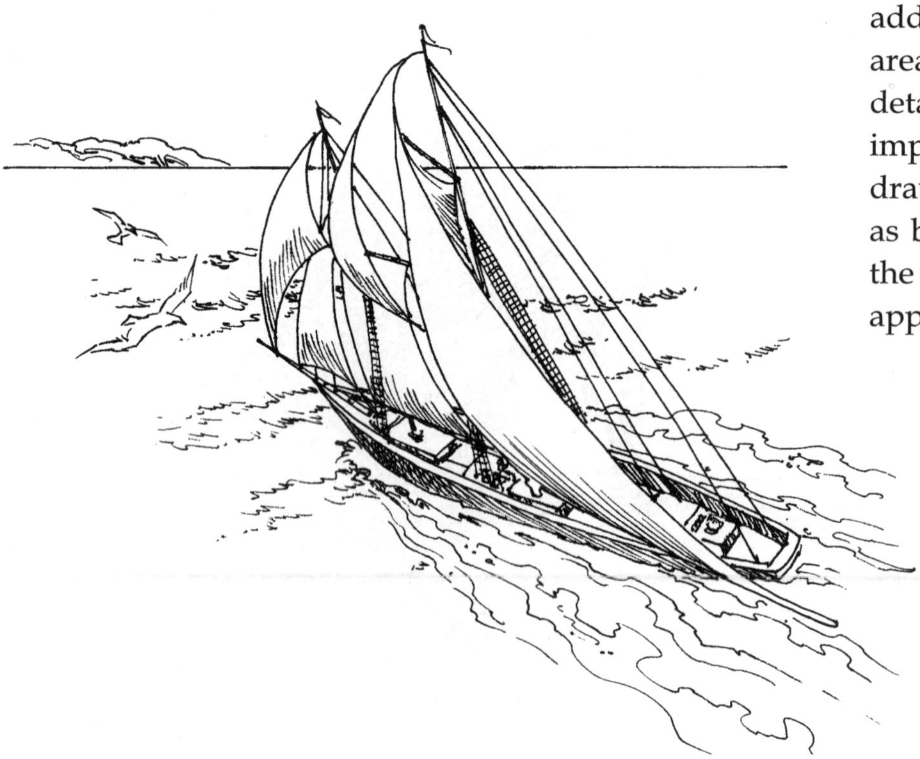

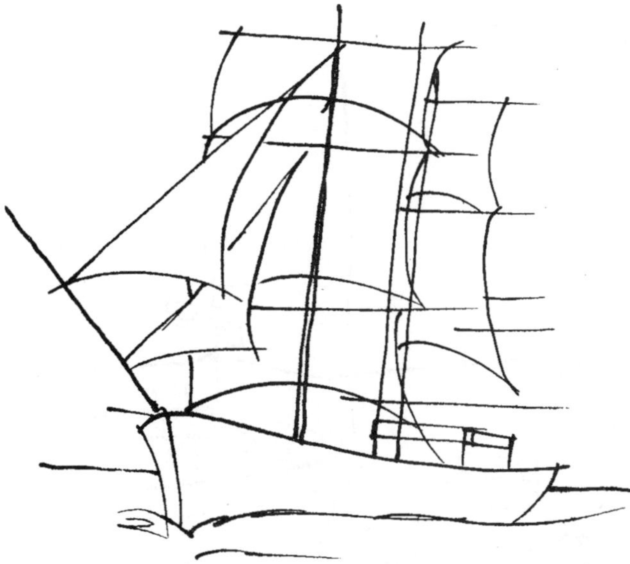

Start with the main parts.

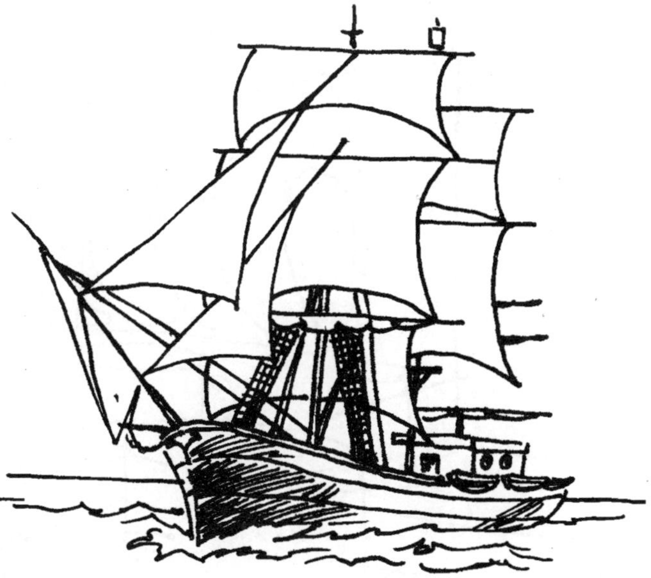

Add total line work.

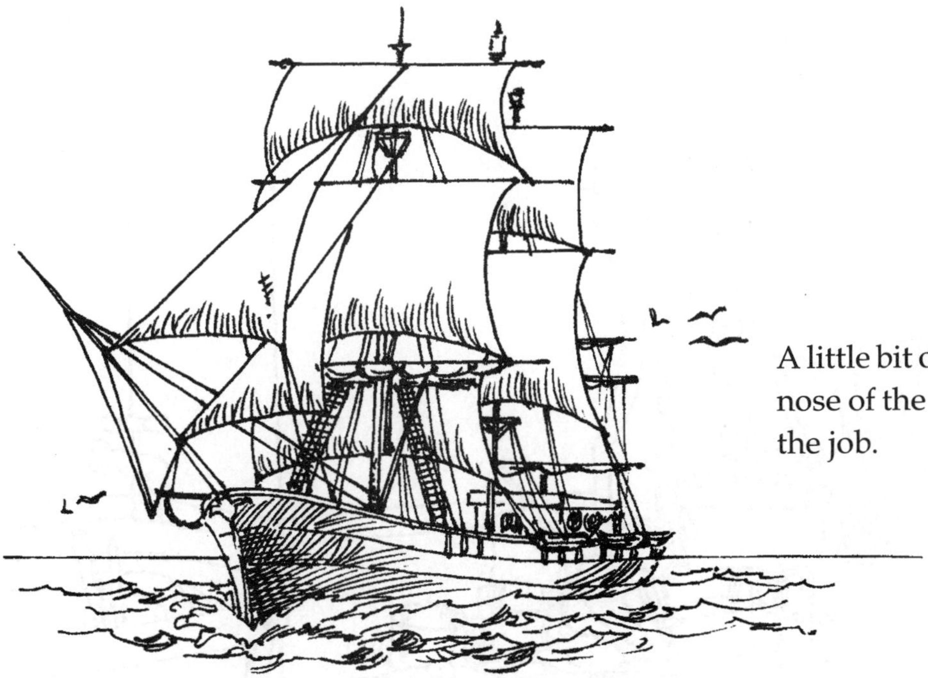

A little bit of shade around the nose of the boat's 'sail' will do the job.

A lone boat floating at the horizon line produces a great dominance over the otherwise blank landscape. But it gives the illusion of vastness of the ocean.

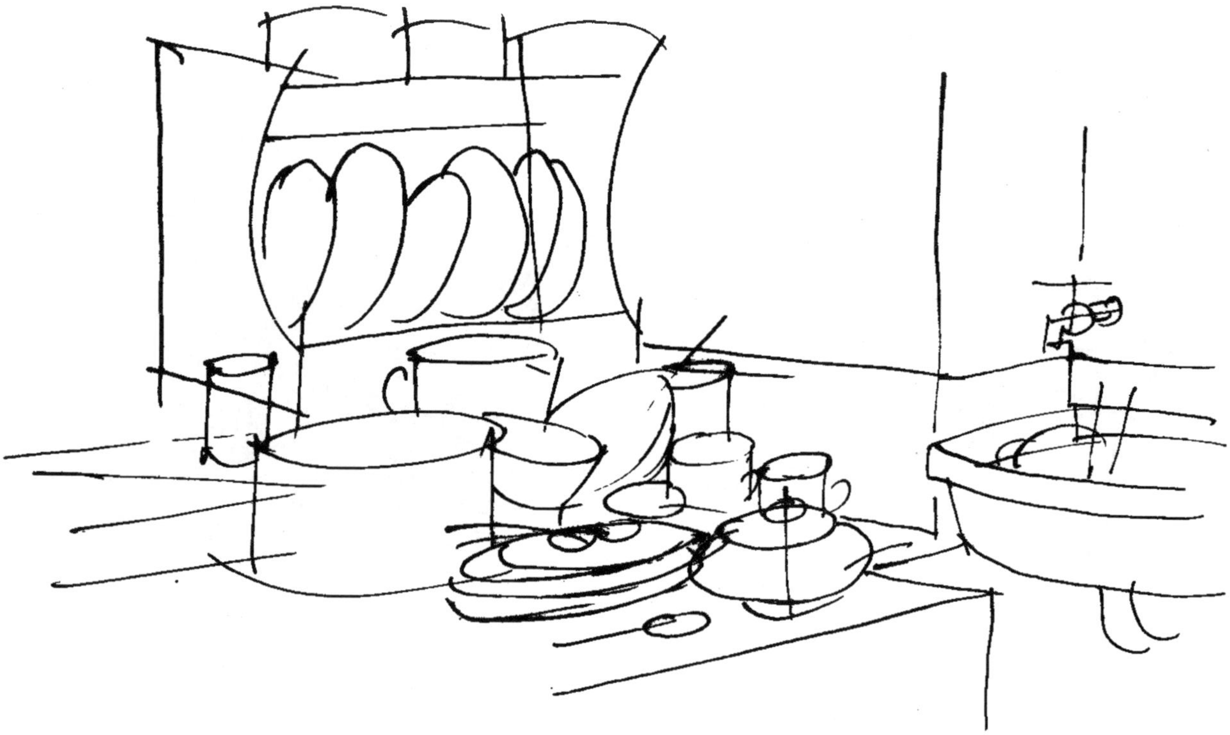

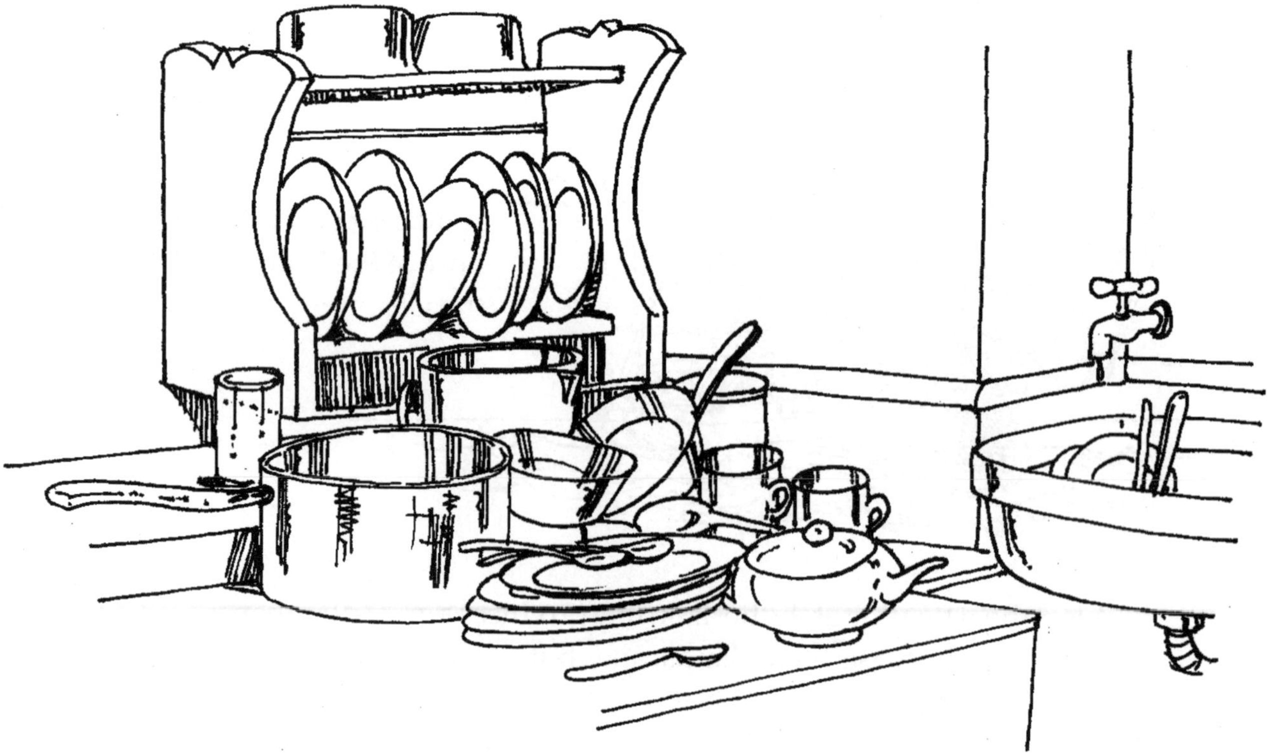

First block the area of body and wings. Then add the lines suggesting grass.

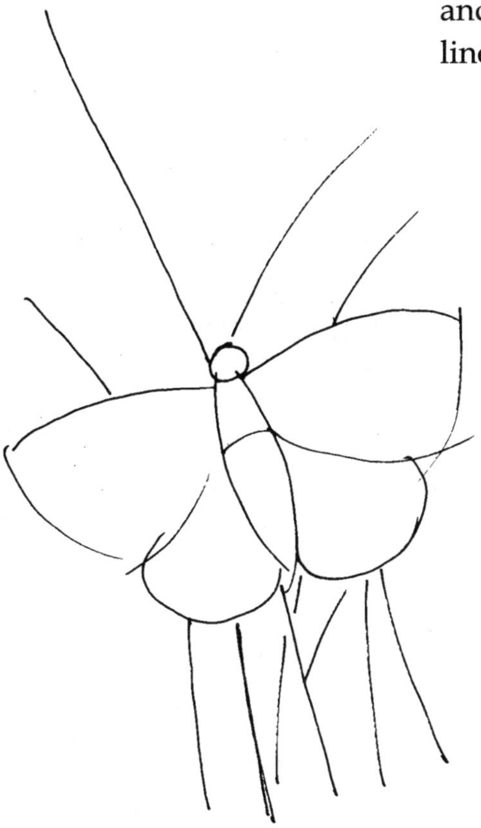

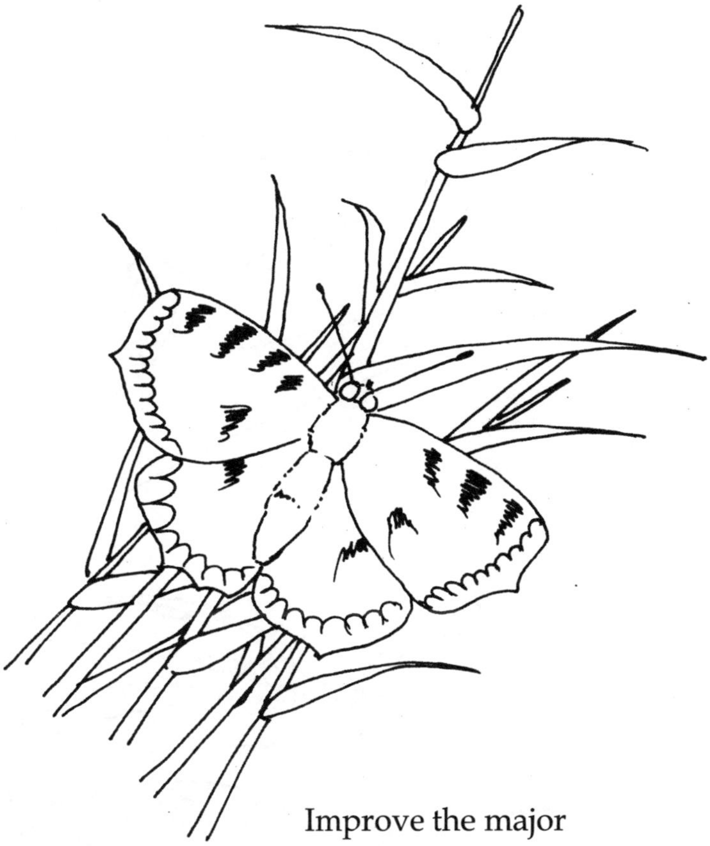

Improve the major texture it has.

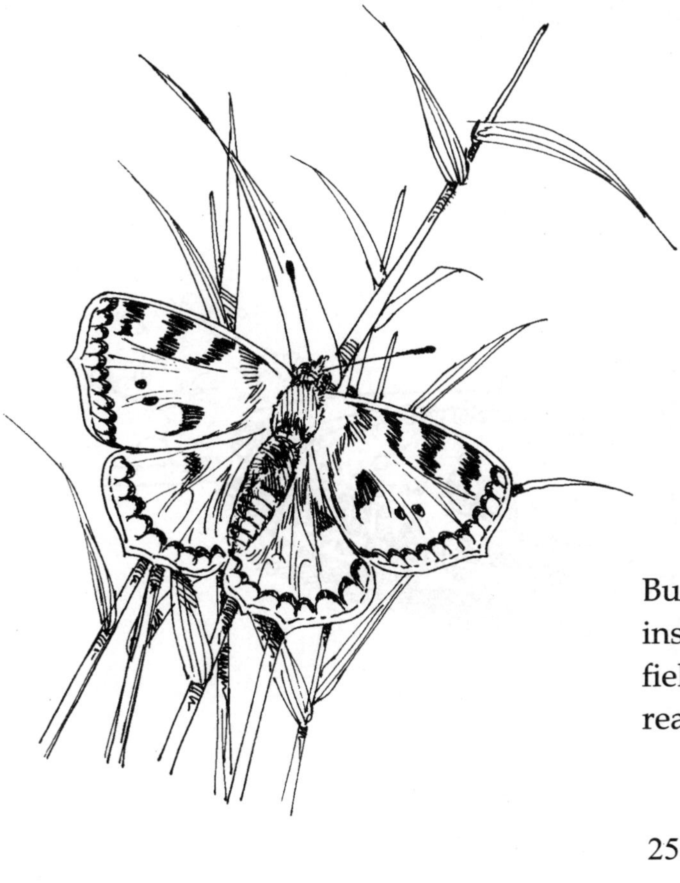

Butterflies are the most beautiful insects. When they fly in the open fields and from bush to bush, it is really pleasing to watch.

When drawing vehicles, draw them in moving state. It will give life to your machine and create a great contrast of hardness and softness.

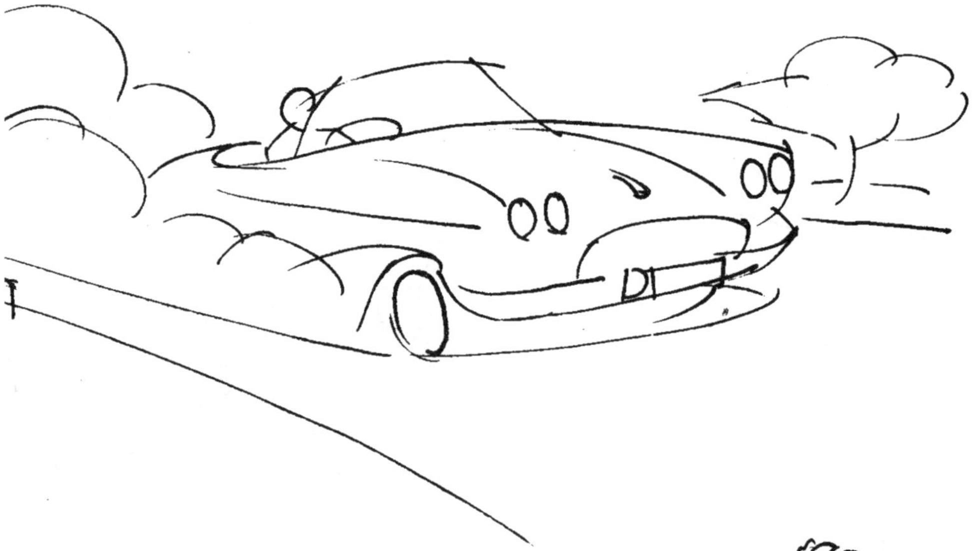

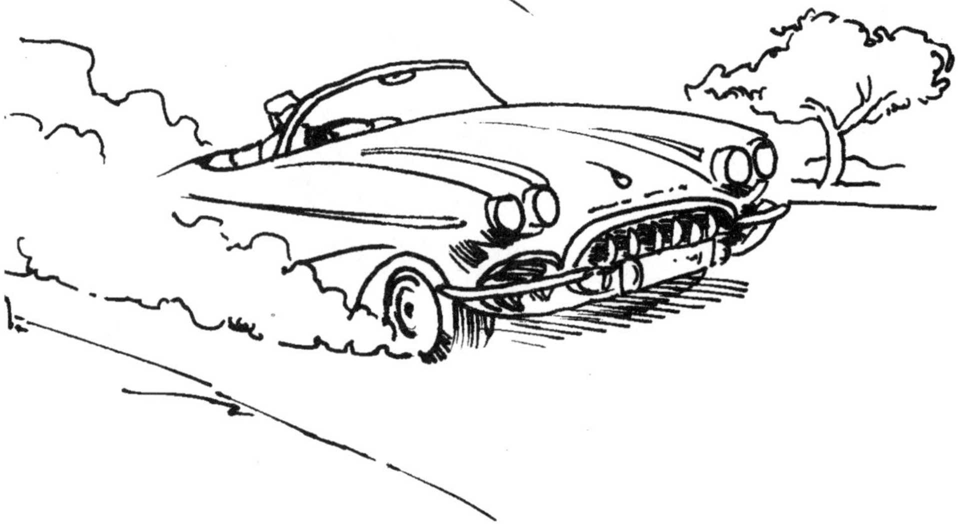

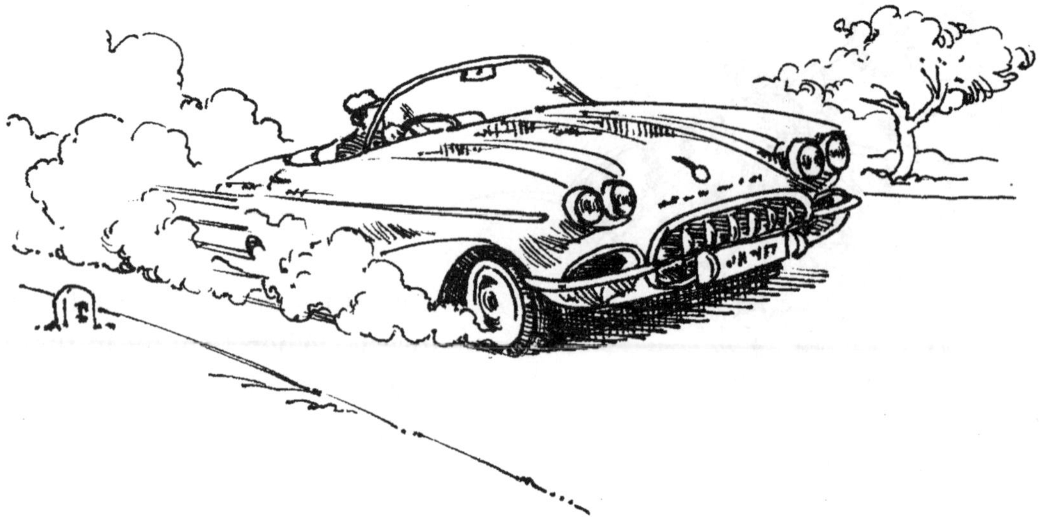

Use straight lines to place the vehicle.

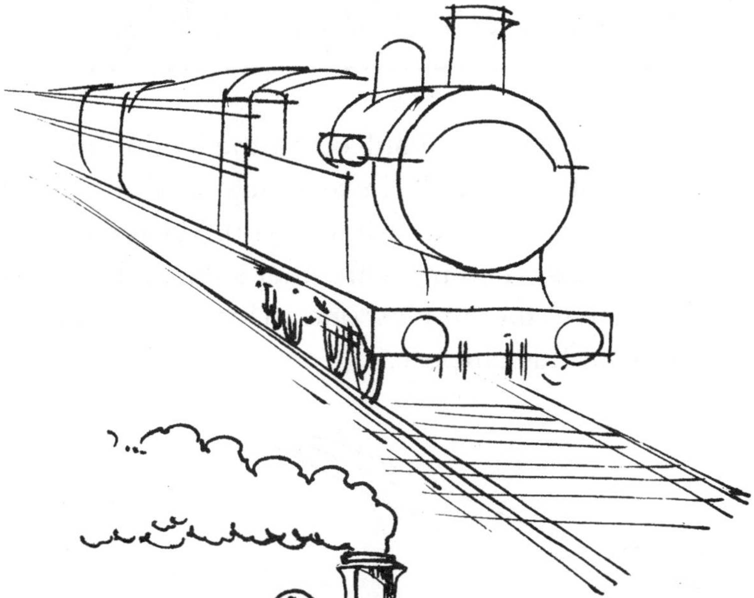

Draw various parts and track.

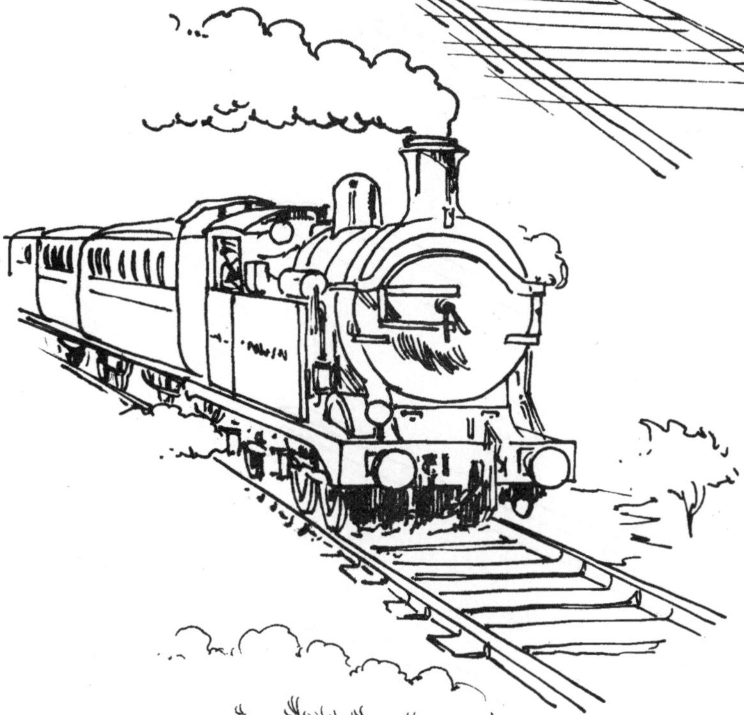

By adding shadows you will be able to lift the train above the tracks.

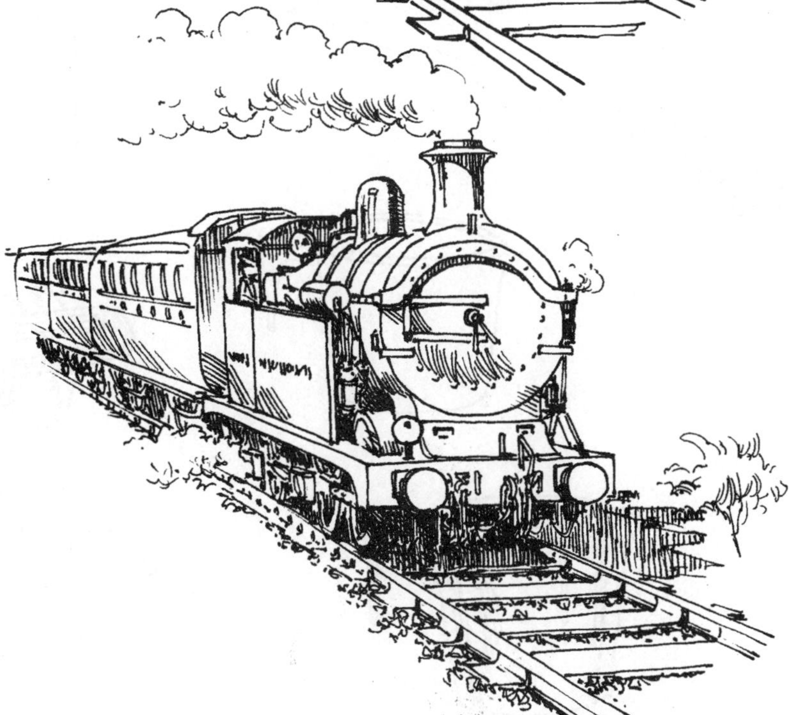

Start with the Simpler Things

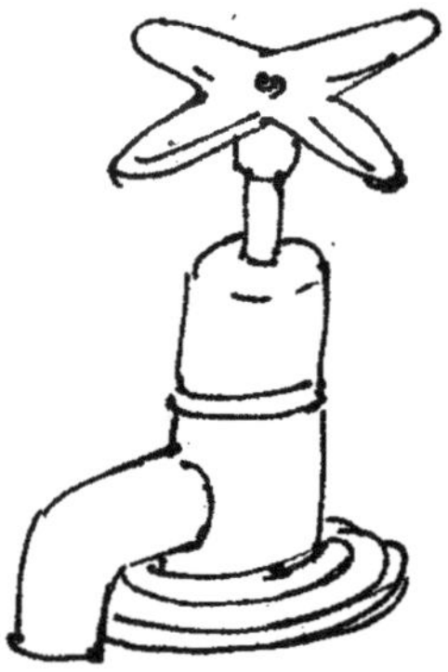

Never choose a difficult subject in the beginning. You will be disappointed if you do. Instead, select a drawing which is very simple and easy according to you. Master it by copying it several times. Then try with other subjects but at least for a week, stick to the simplest ones. This book contains many drawings for this purpose.

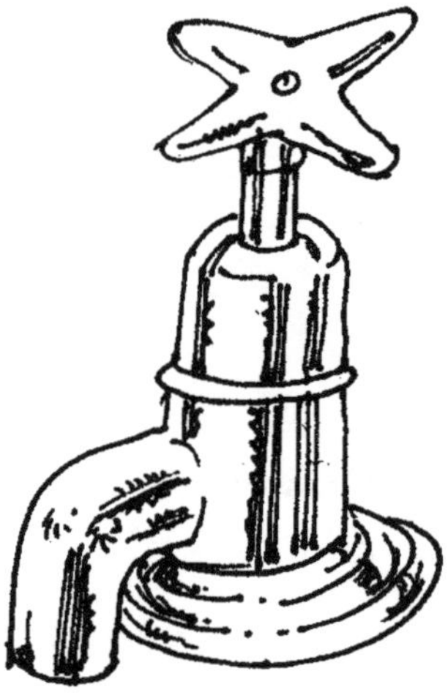

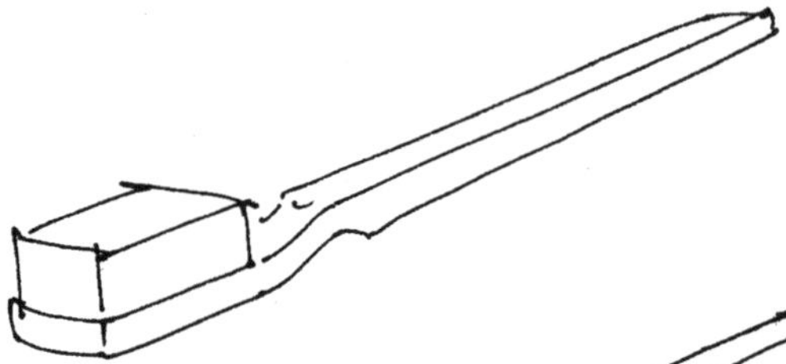

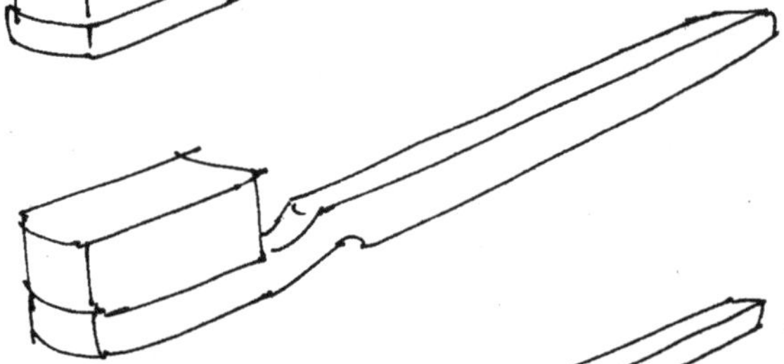

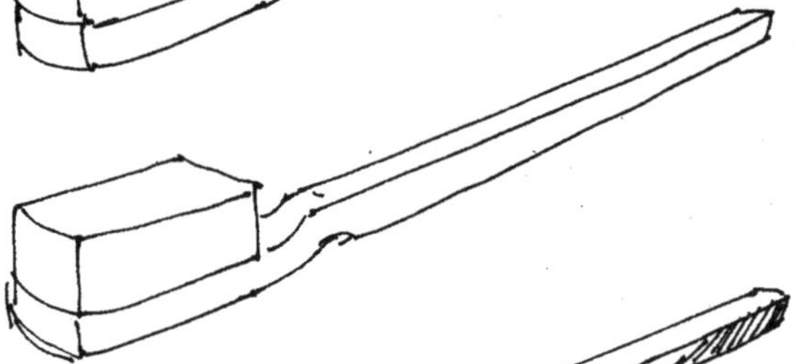

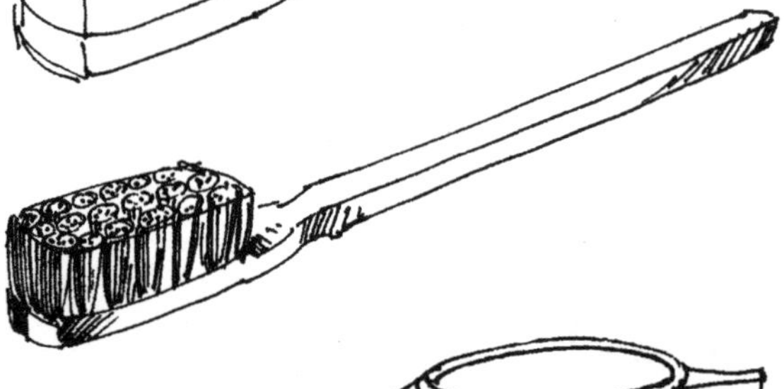

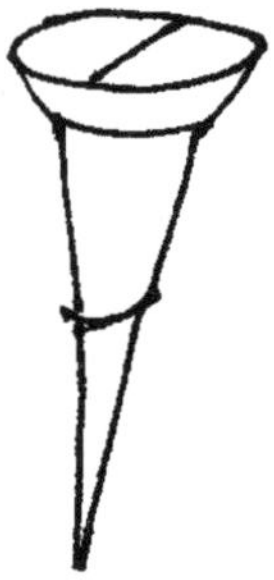

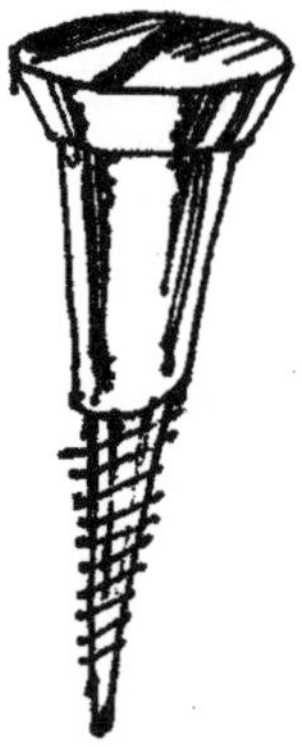

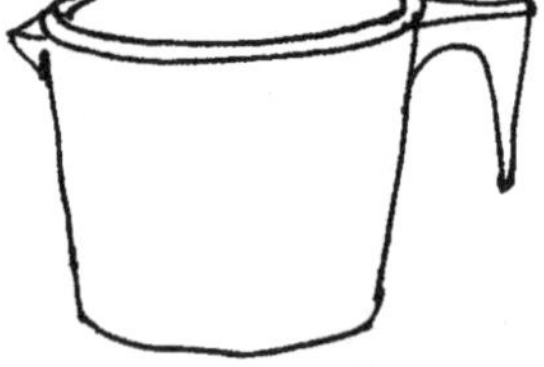

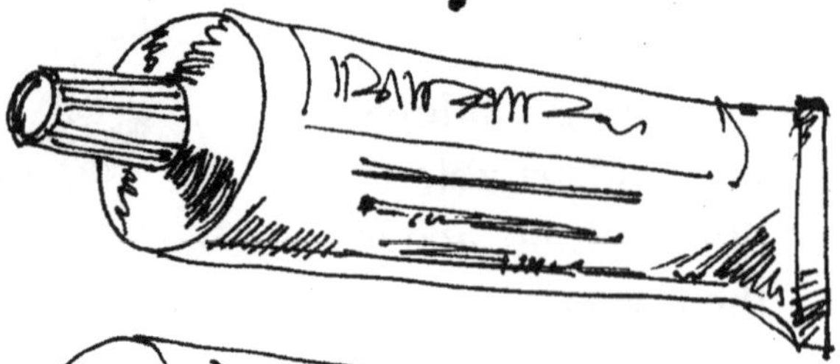

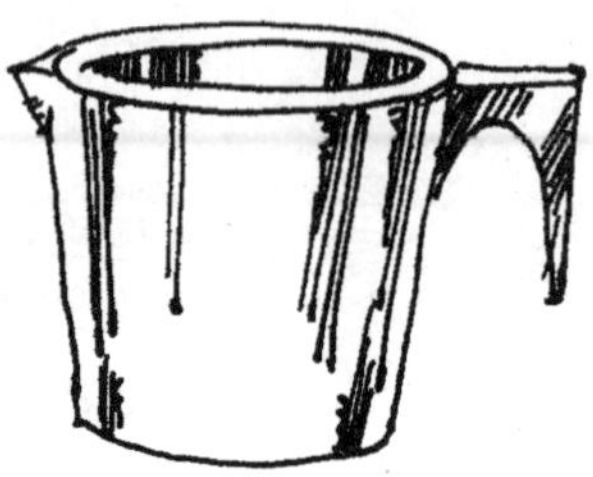

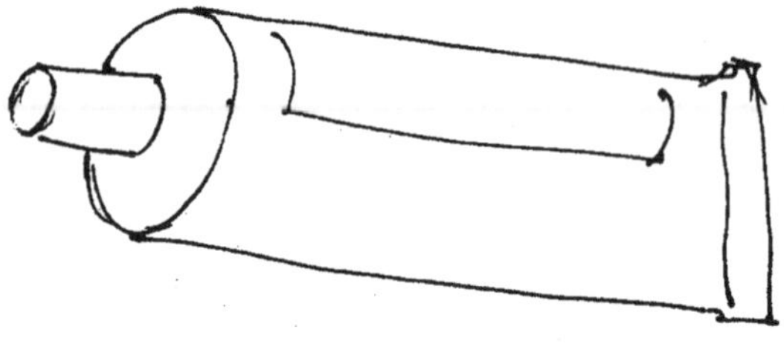

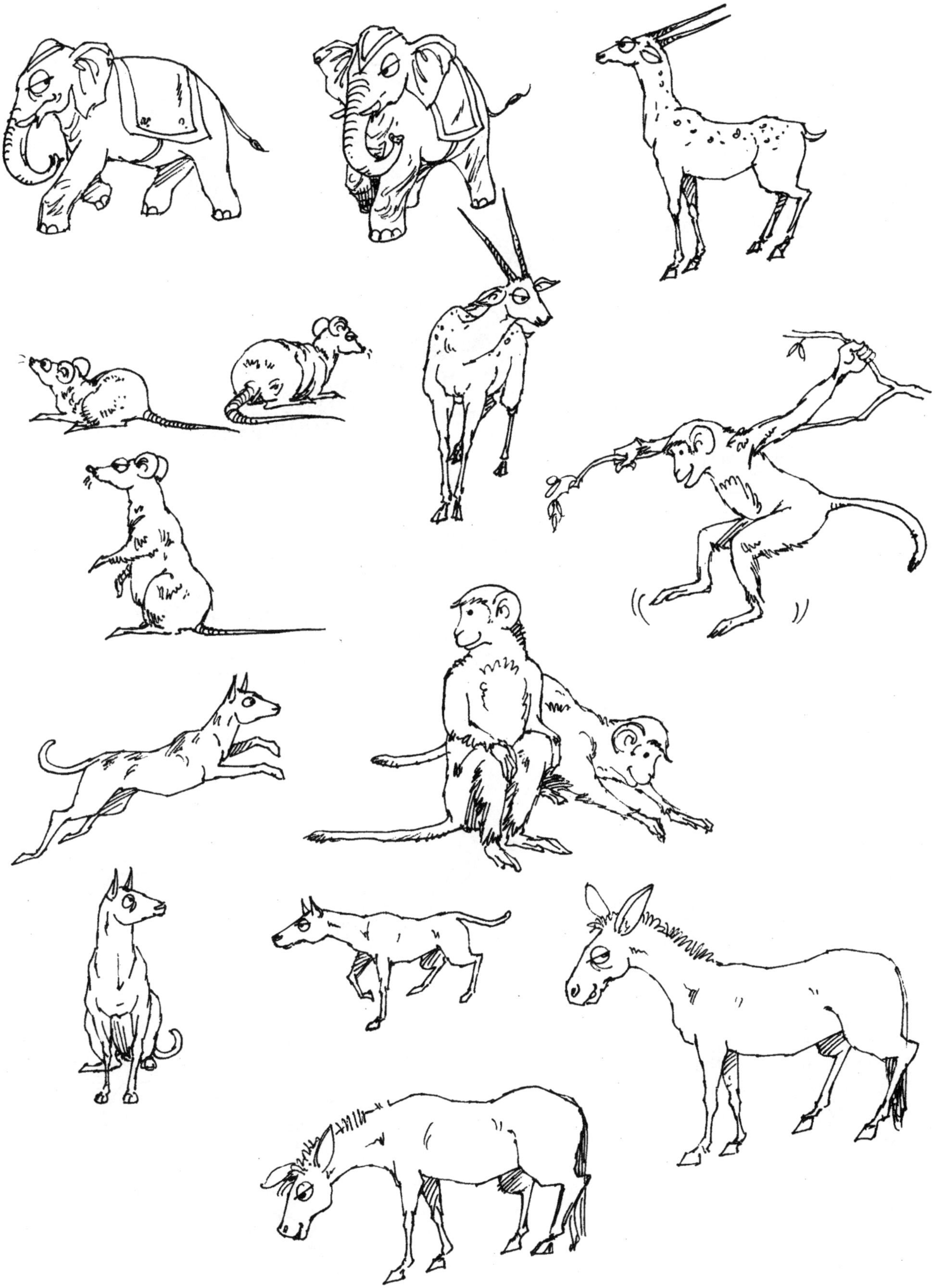

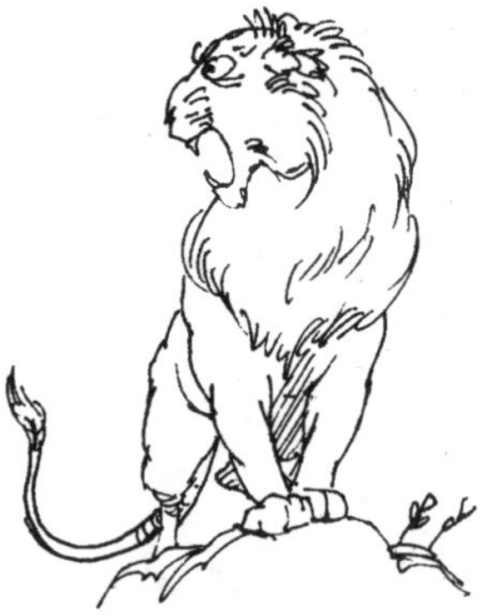

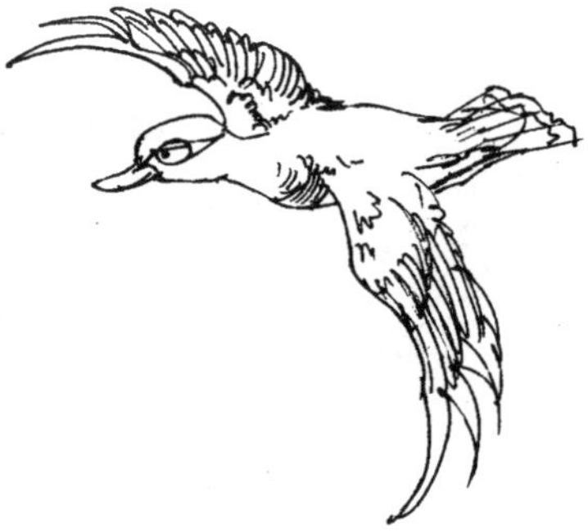

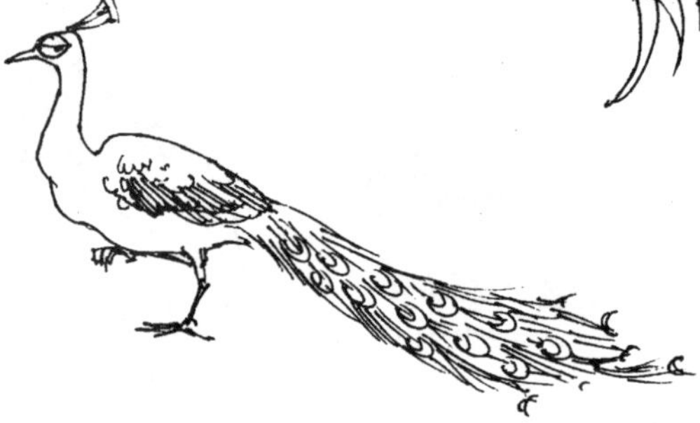

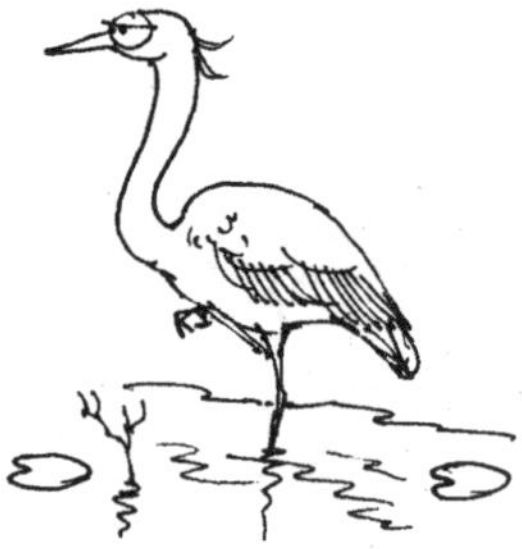

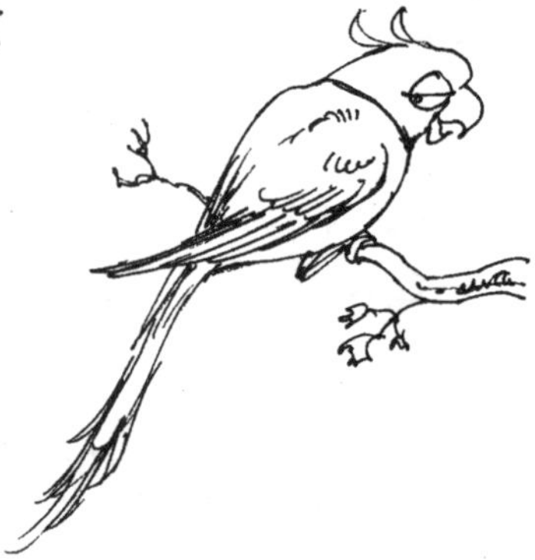

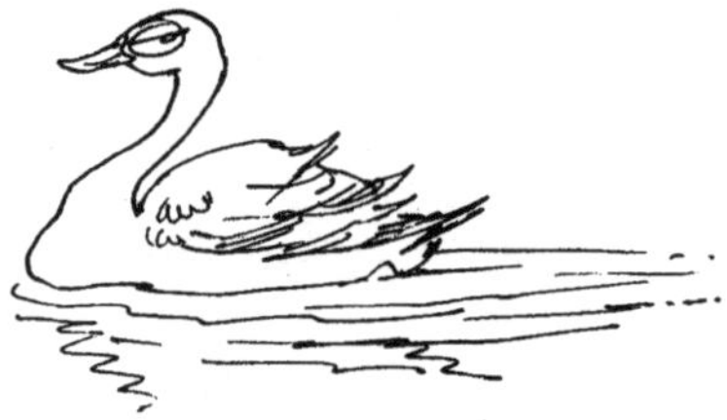

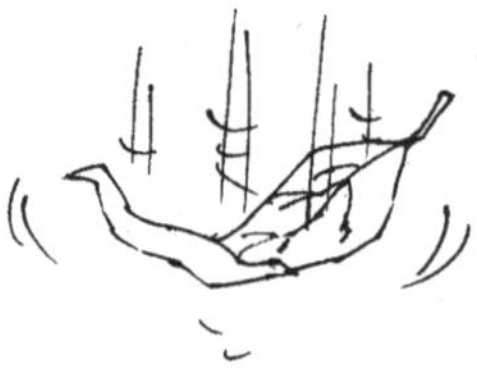

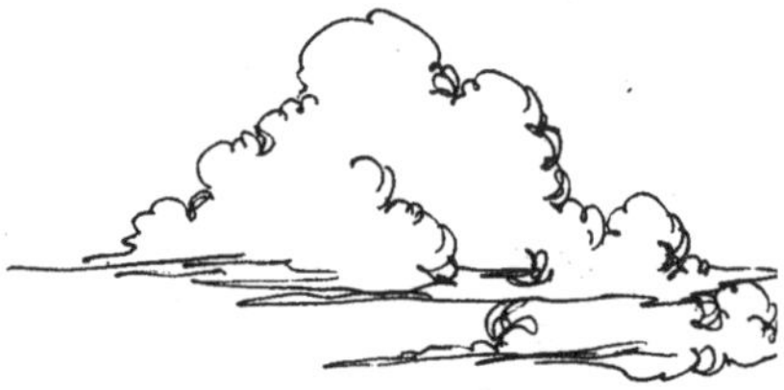

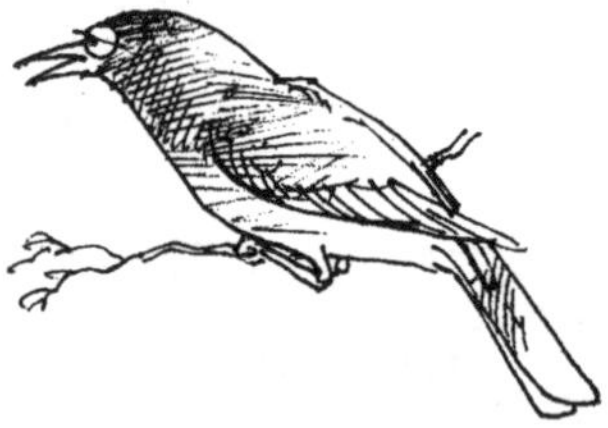

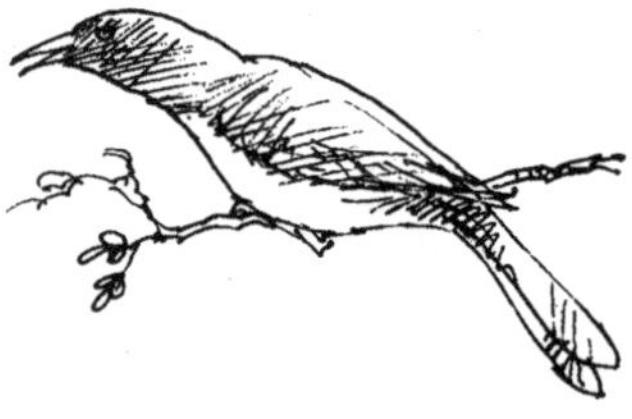

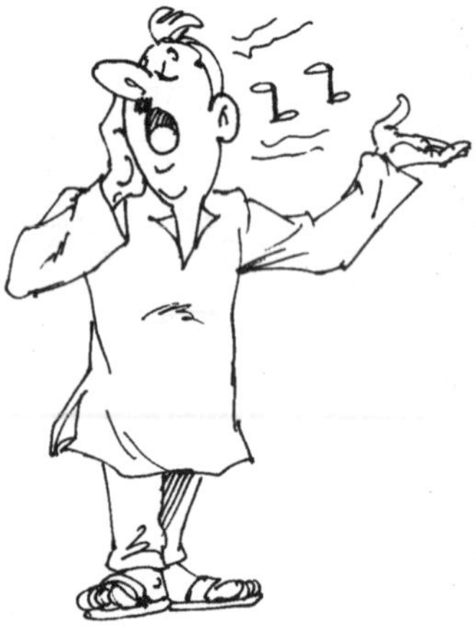

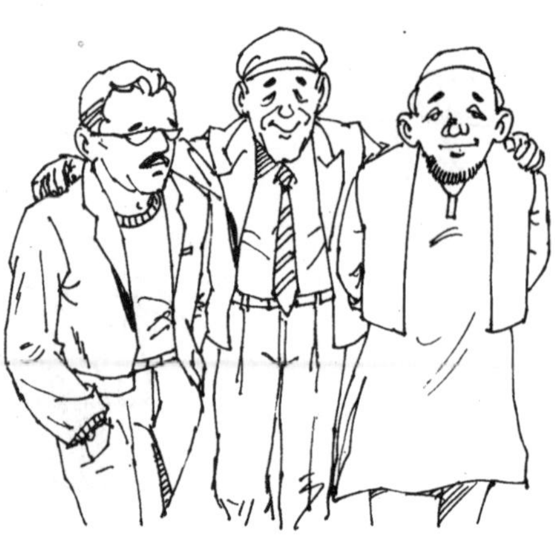

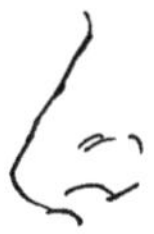
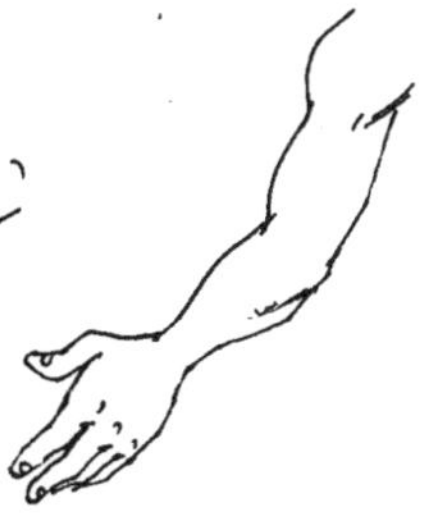
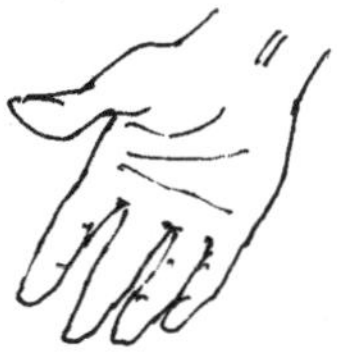
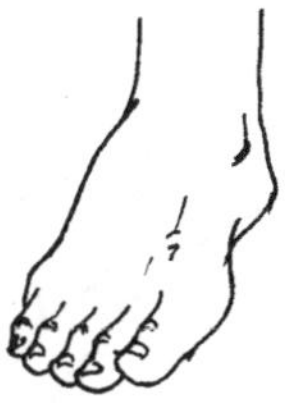
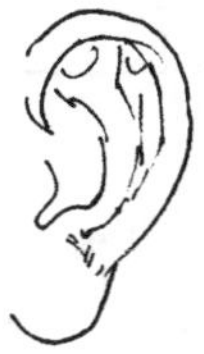
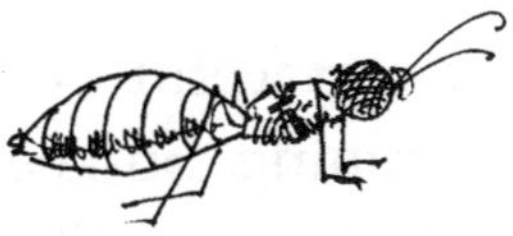
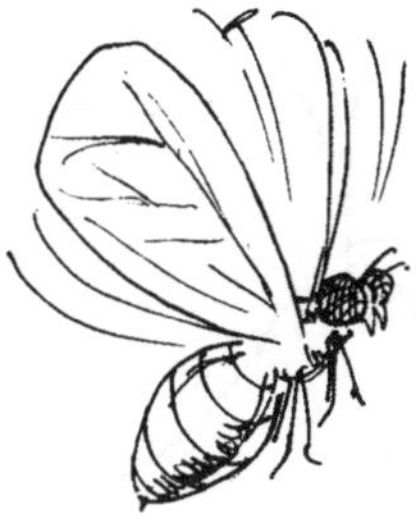
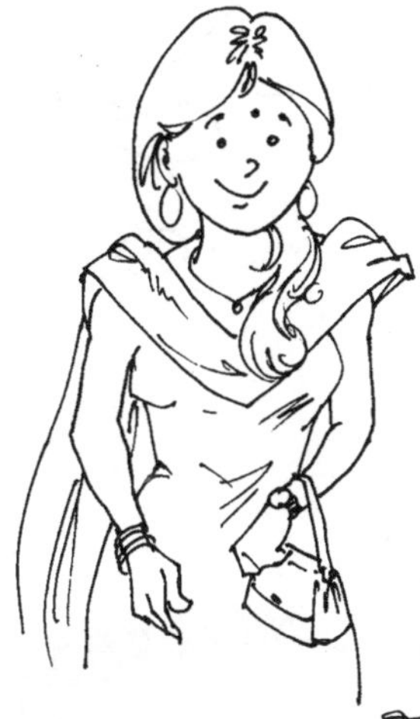
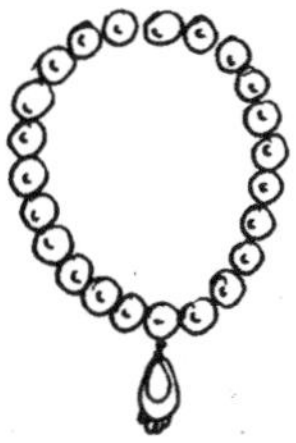
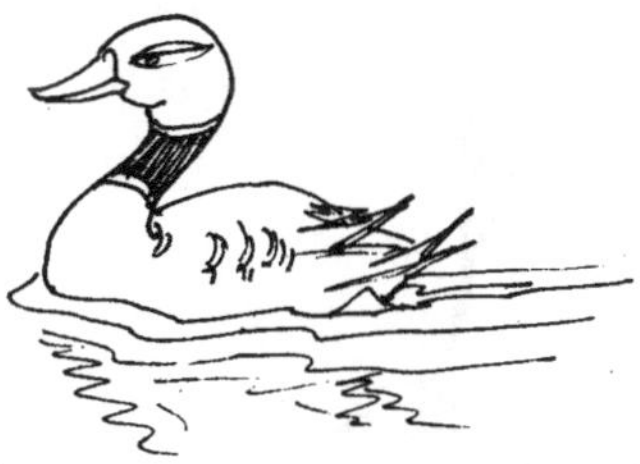
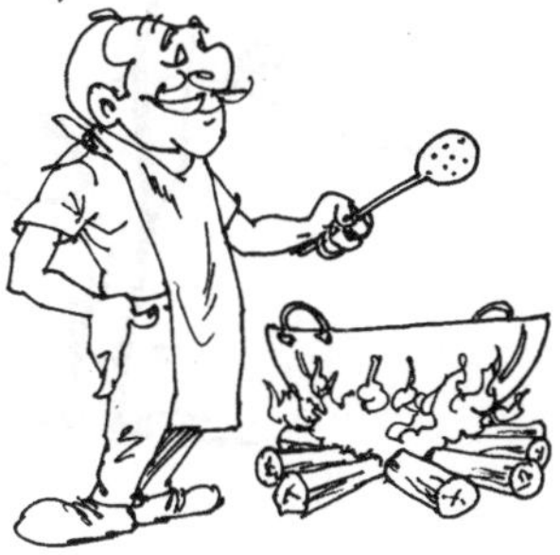
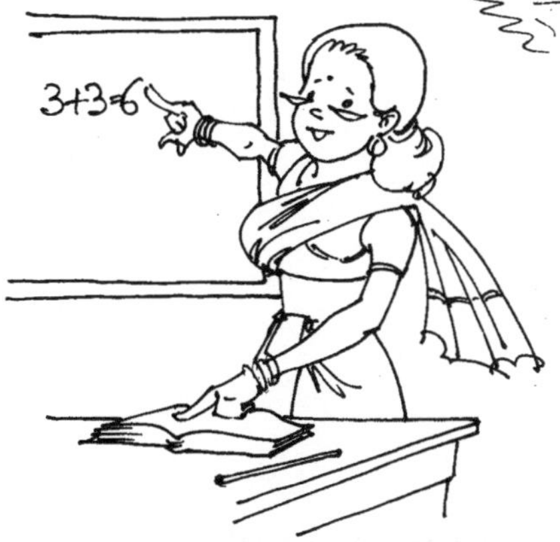
3+3=6
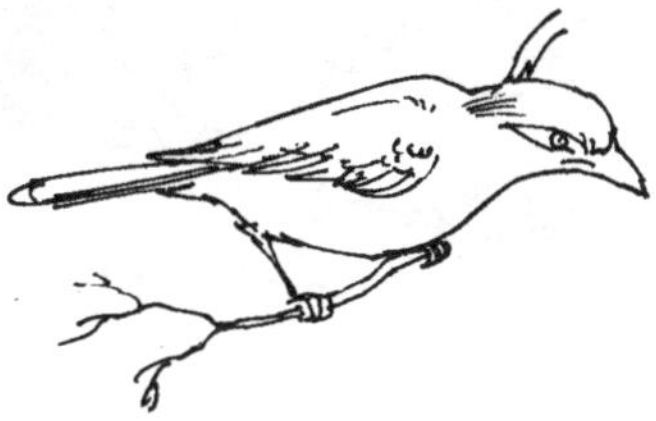
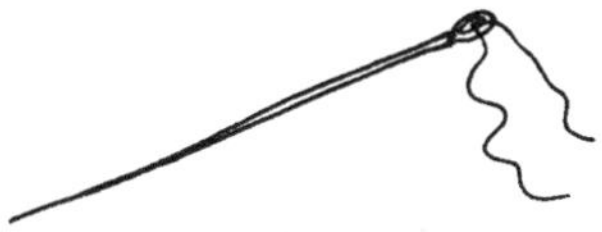
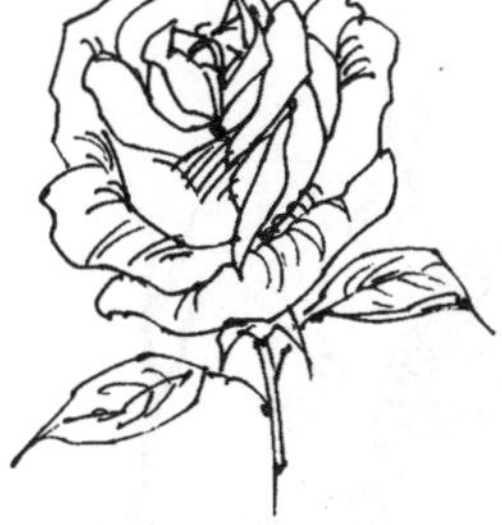
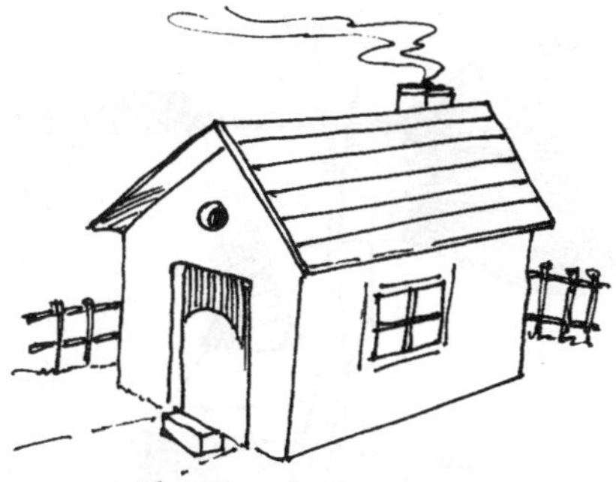
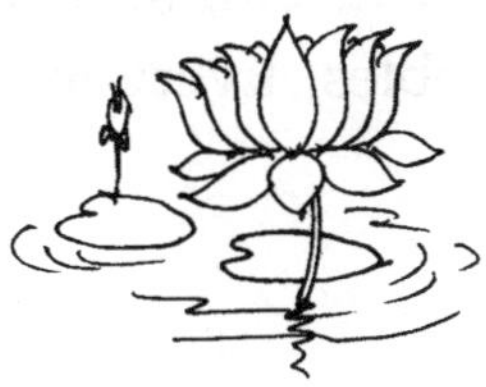

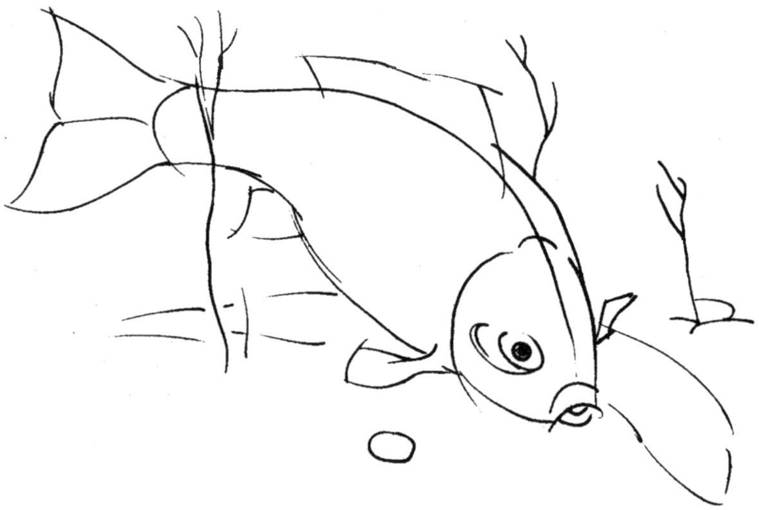

A fish has graceful curvatures when swimming. So keep those shades as little as possible.

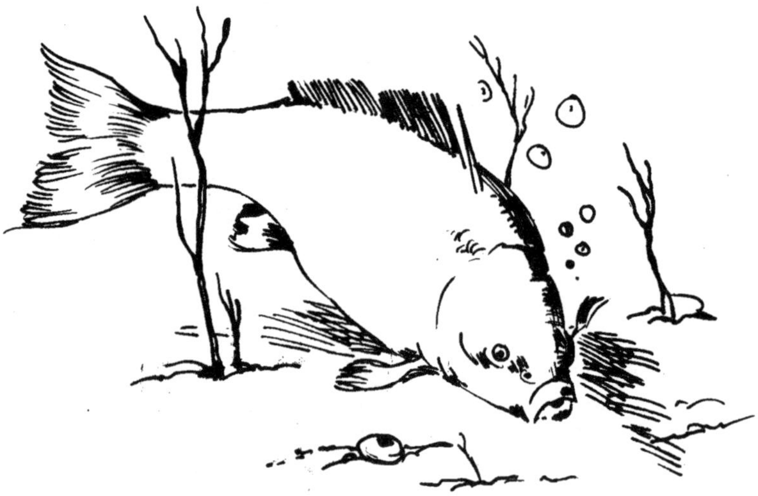

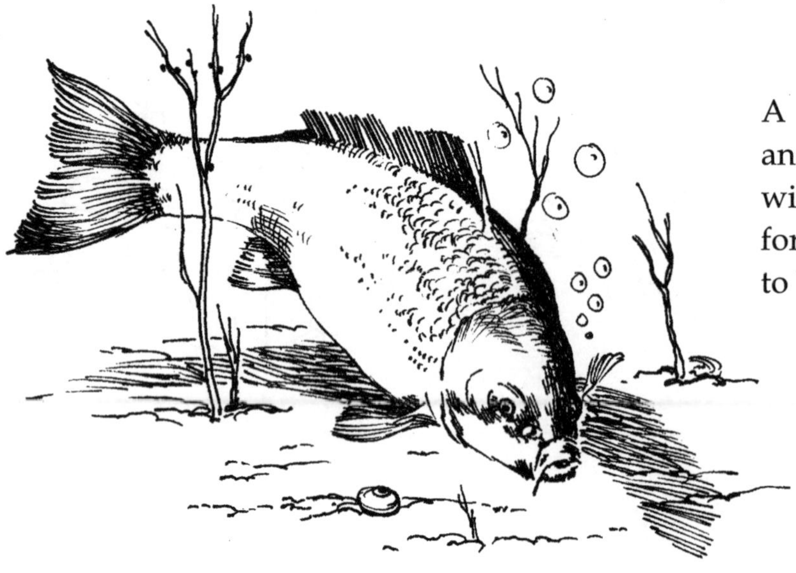

A shadow beneath the creature and some long curved line detail will put life in it. Oh, and don't forget the bubbles. Everyone has to breathe.

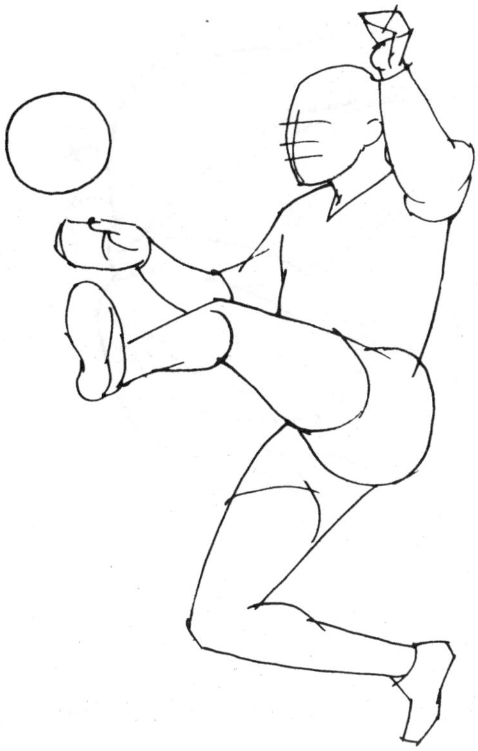

Correctly place the angles of the legs and body with that of the ball.

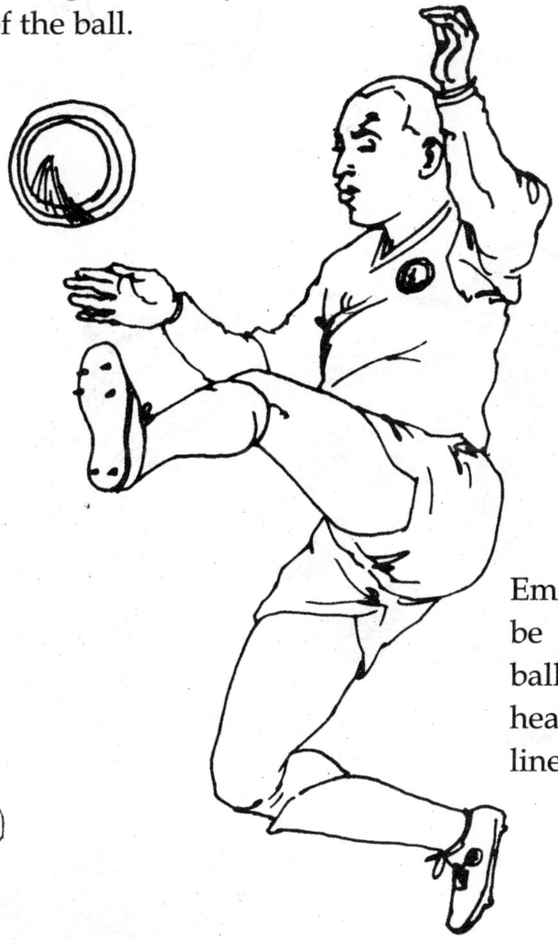

Emphasis should be on left shoe, ball and the head. Add major line work.

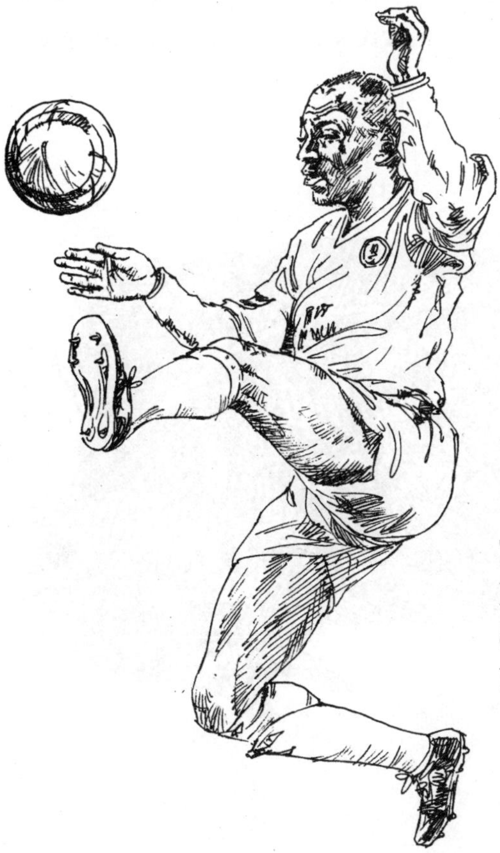

Take a jump and kick it hard. A figure in motion is exciting to draw. Put details but fewer shades.

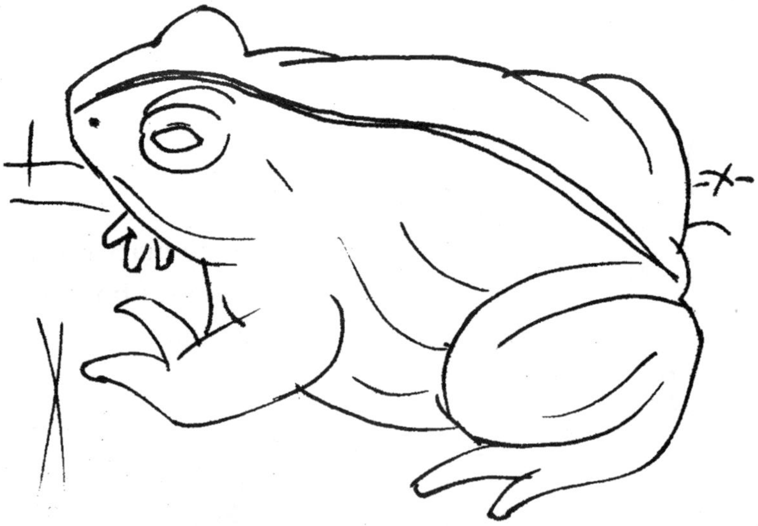

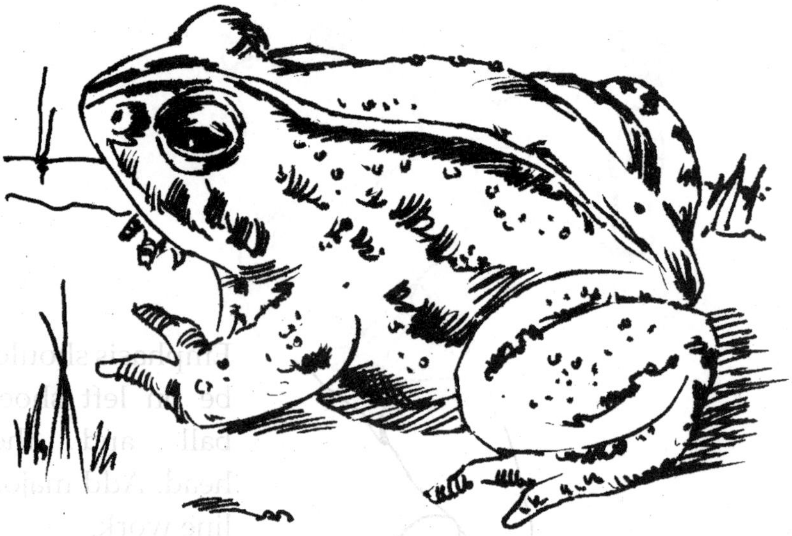

Ever heard about the frog view? It is when you are in the water up to neck deep and earth is at your eye level. You can see the vast sky and small flying birds. So, let's croak and jump. Shall we?

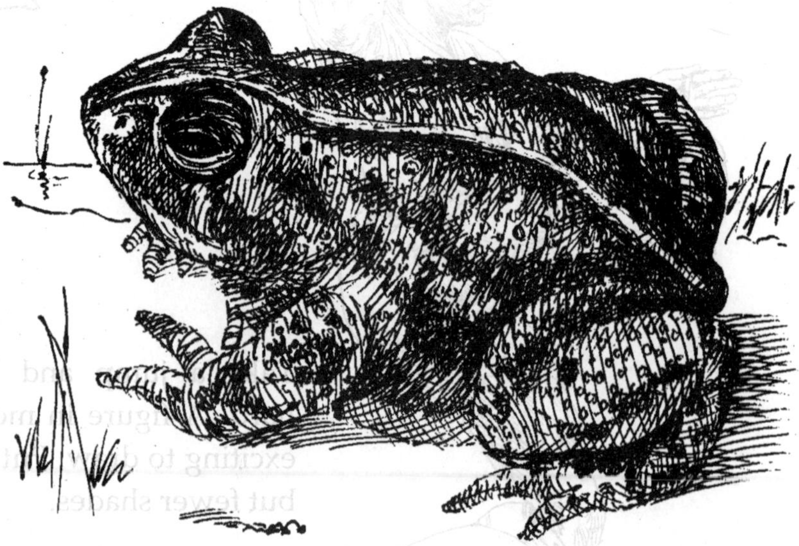

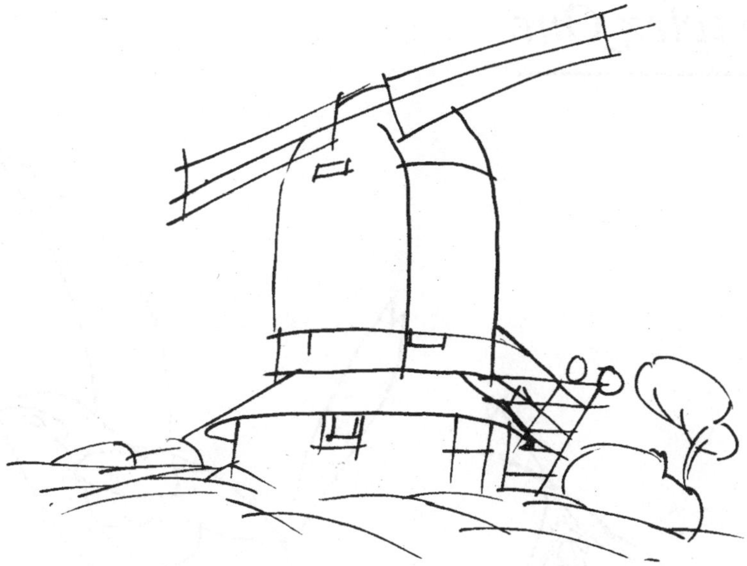

Some of the old structures have more potential for a good drawing than the new ones. A discarded mill in the European countryside presents an interesting view.

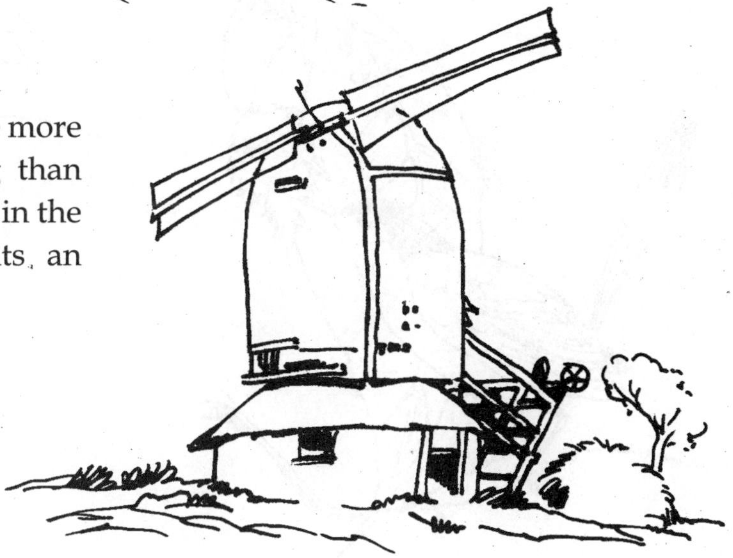

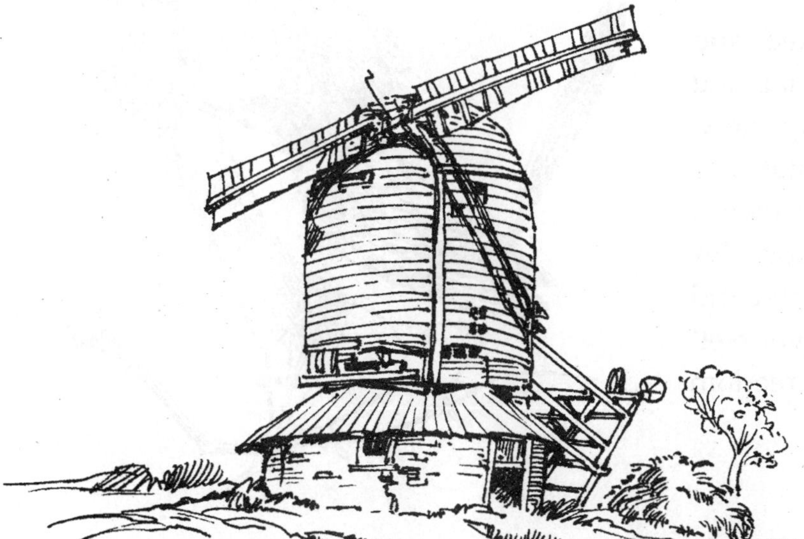

Now the Complex One

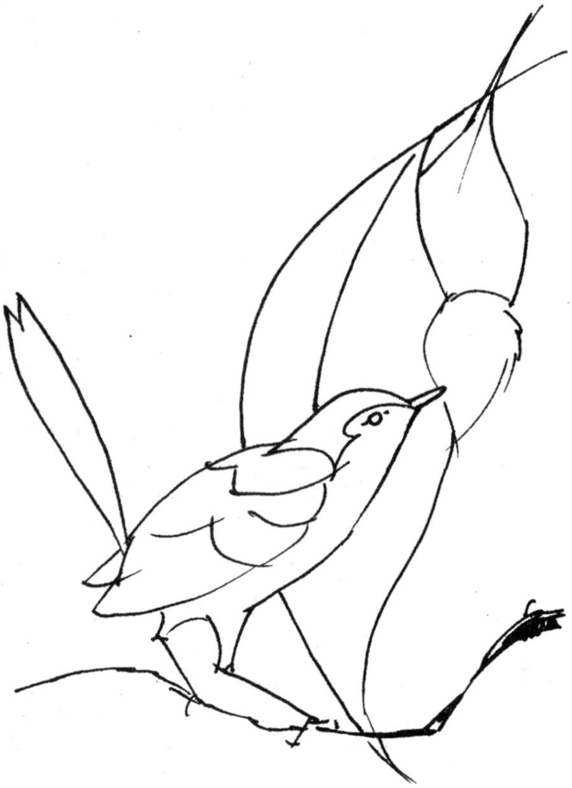

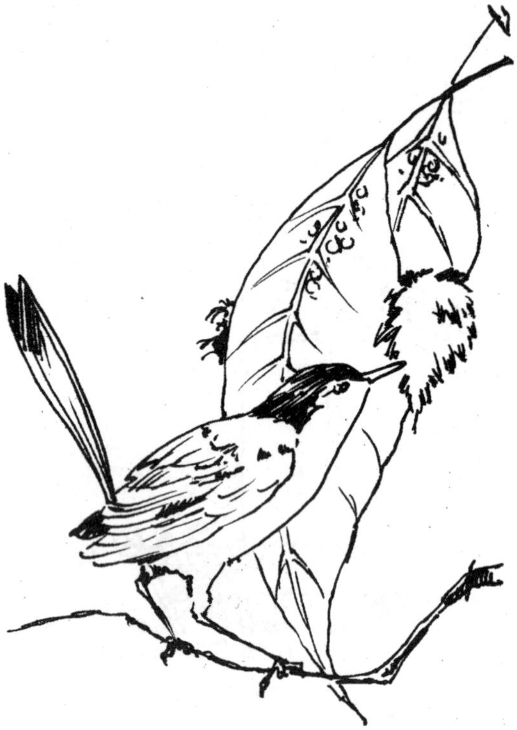

As your hand gets relaxed and the movement more casual and fluent, try complex drawings now. We would advise here that you should not quit at least for a week even you do not succeed. Complex sketches are difficult to master and may take some time. Give yourself some space and time. Freedom will follow automatically.

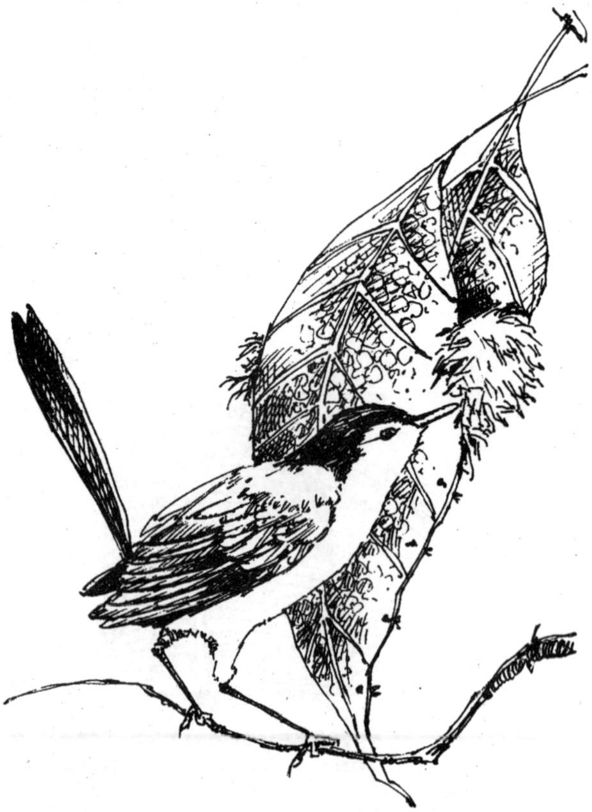

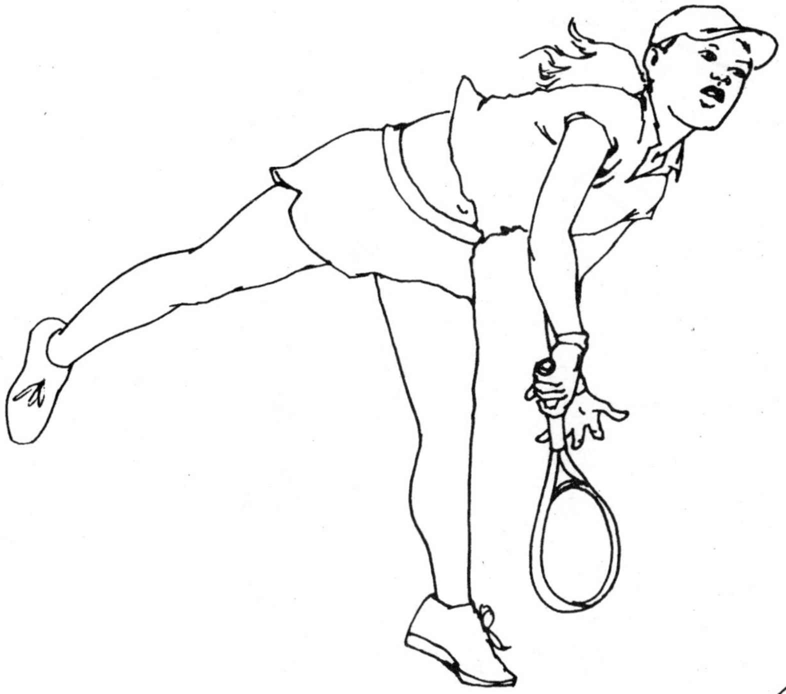

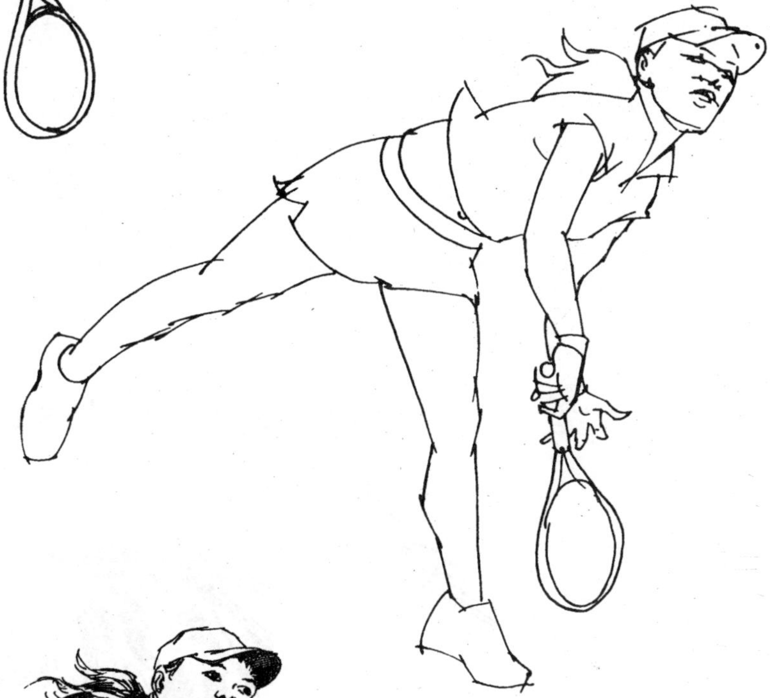

When drawing female figures, stick to the minimum shade.

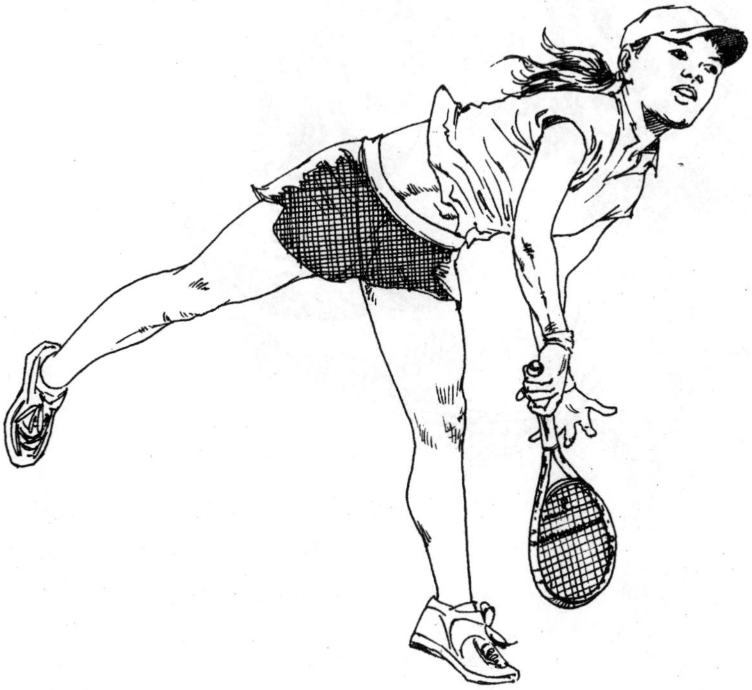

A simple line work will keep it soft and feminine.

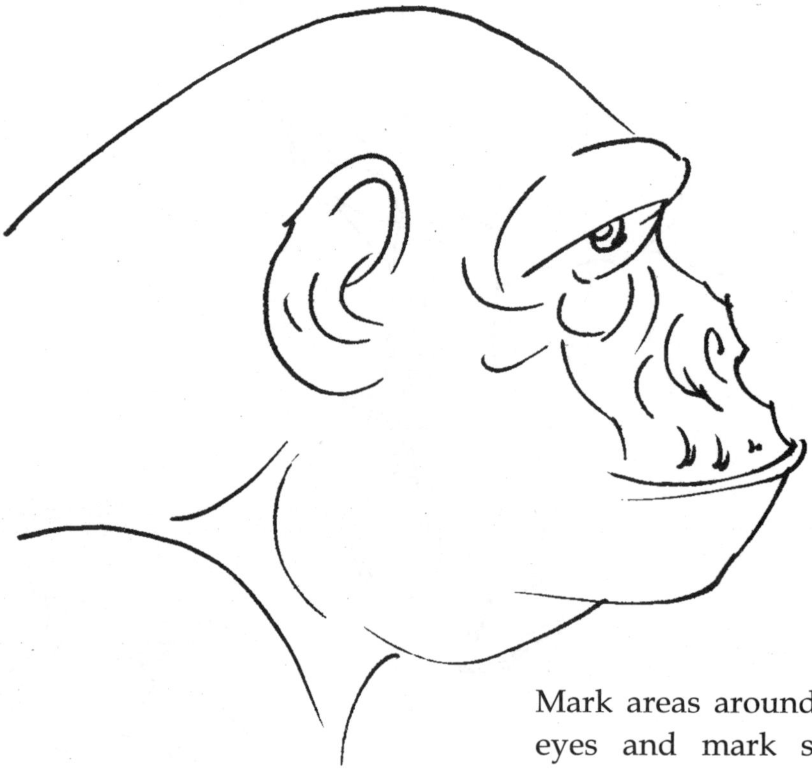

Mark areas around the eyes and mark some main sections.

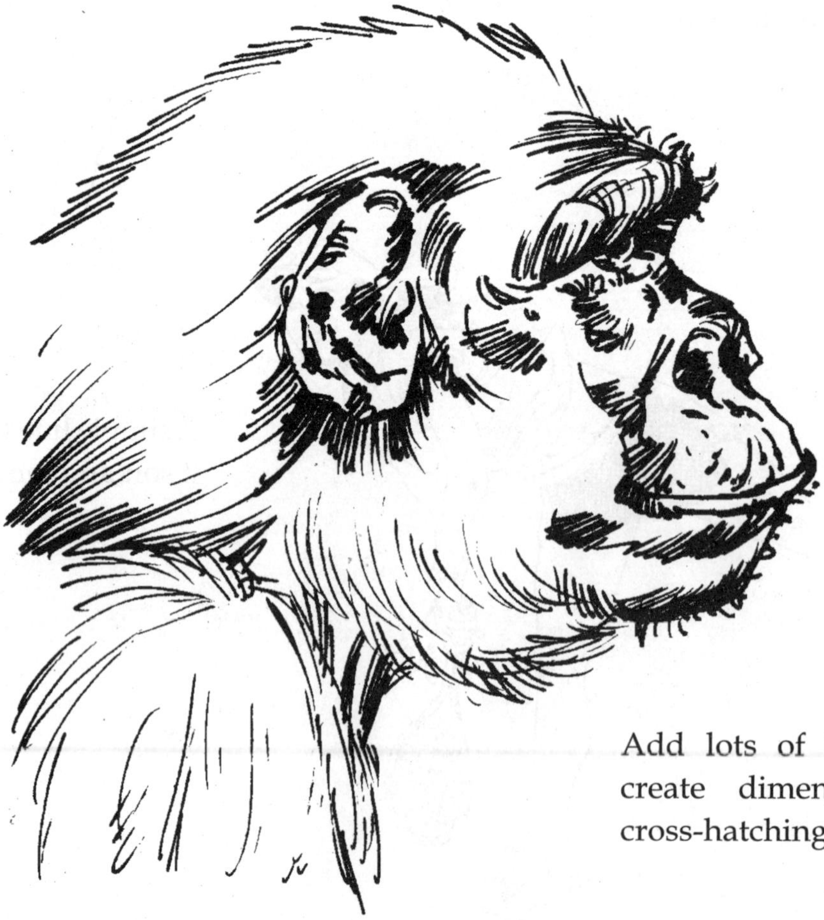

Add lots of hairs and create dimensions by cross-hatching.

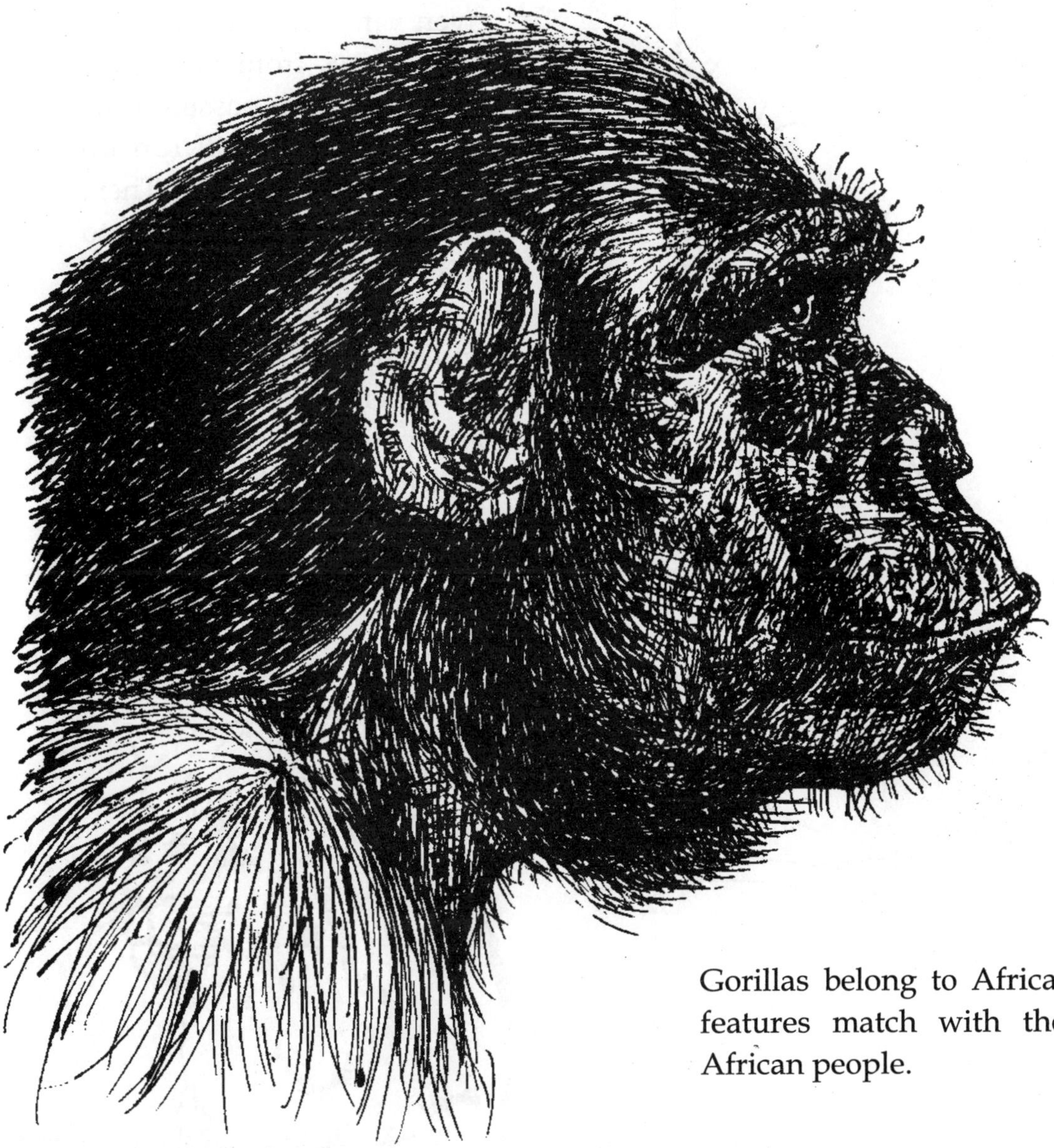

Gorillas belong to Africa. It's facial features match with those of the African people.

At Last, the Challenge

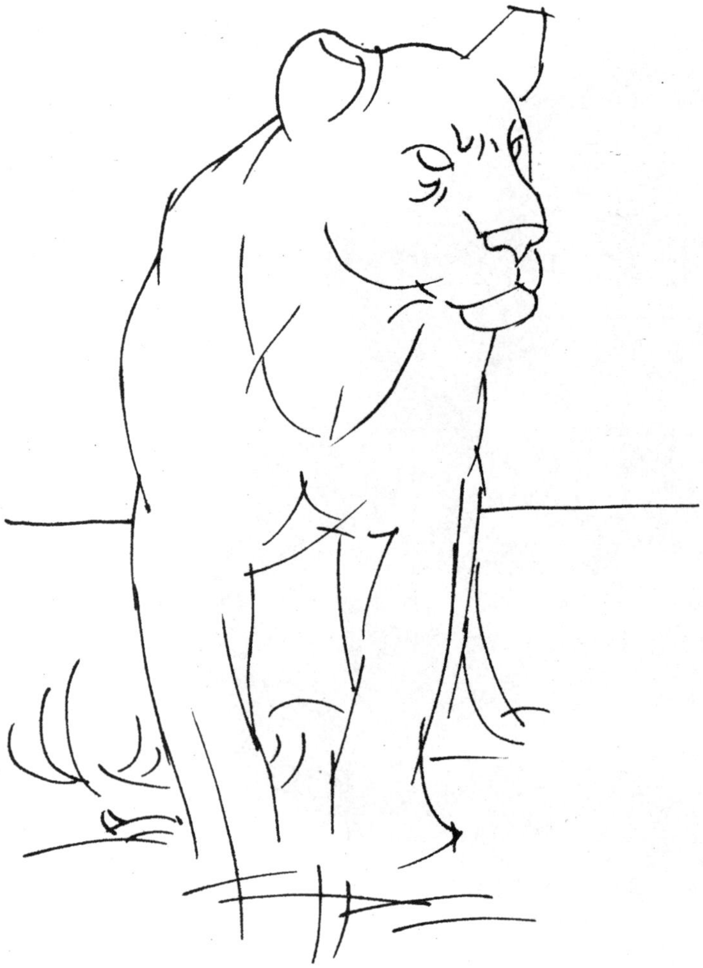

Just keep copying the pictures given in this book and similar ones from your own collection. With passing time and stages, you will run up the stairs of confidence. Then, some day, you will like to draw something challenging and not so easy to achieve. And here lies the pleasure and excitement. We assure you once you do it, you will try it again and again on various subjects. So the journey will begin... journey to become an artist.

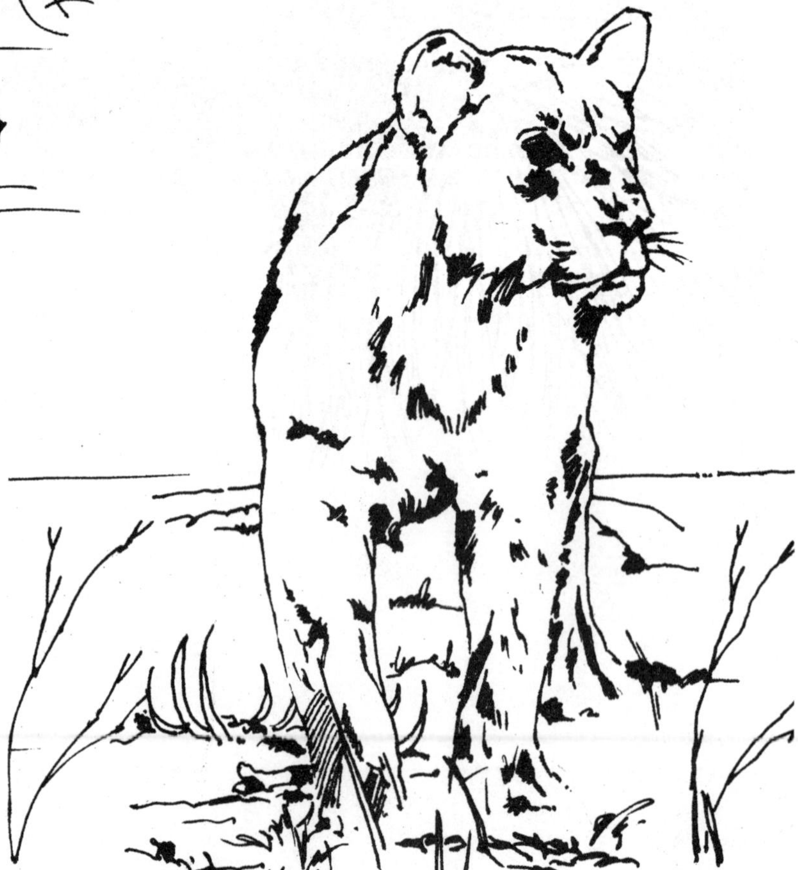

A lioness in the vast plains of Africa. Look in the eyes closely and you will feel the aggression and killer instincts.

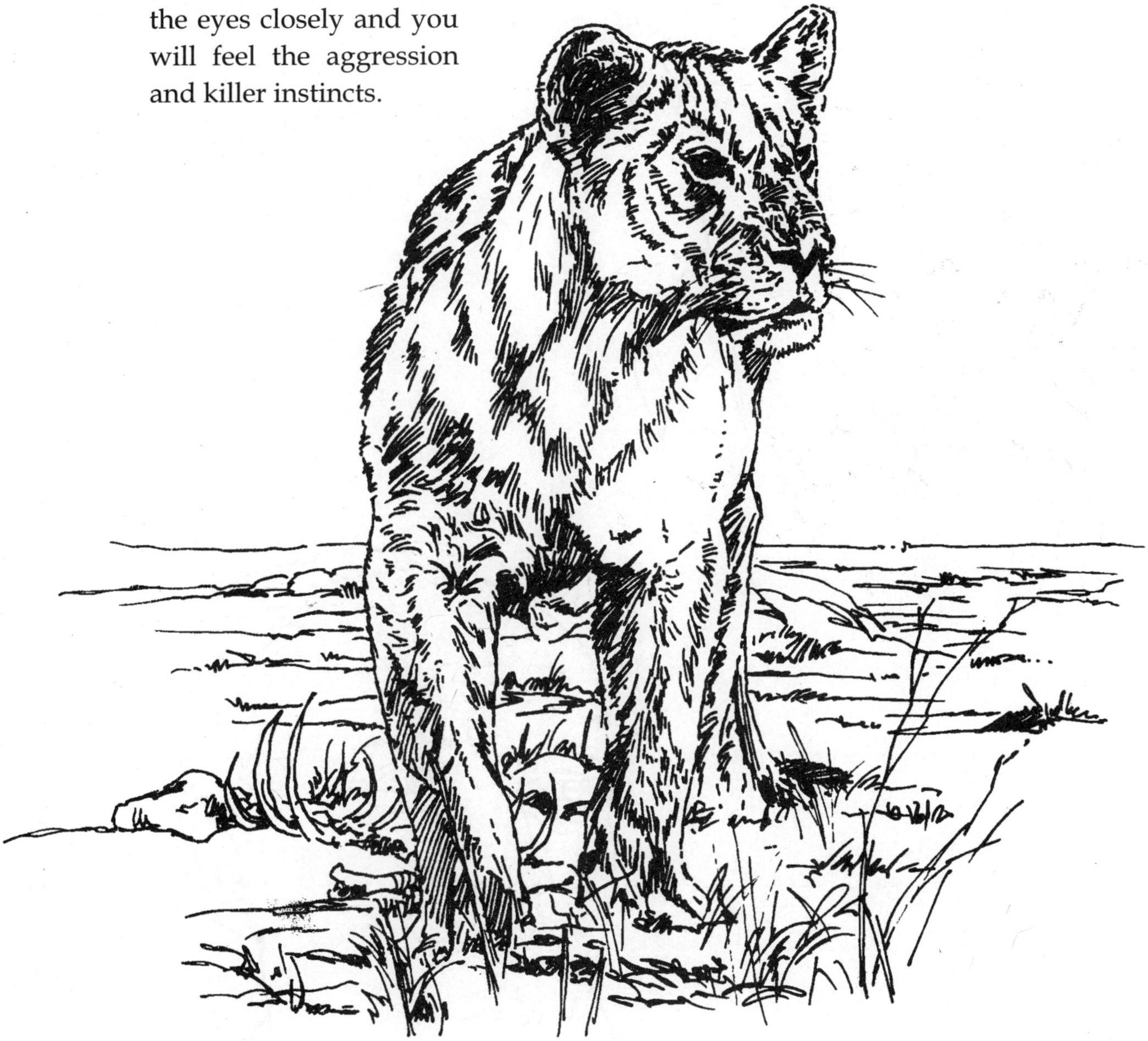

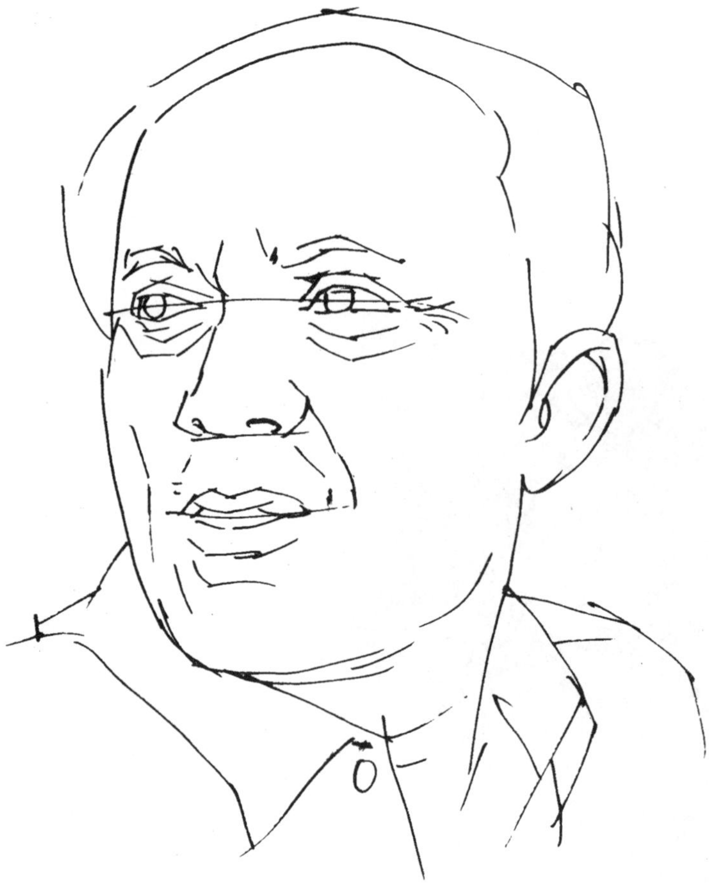

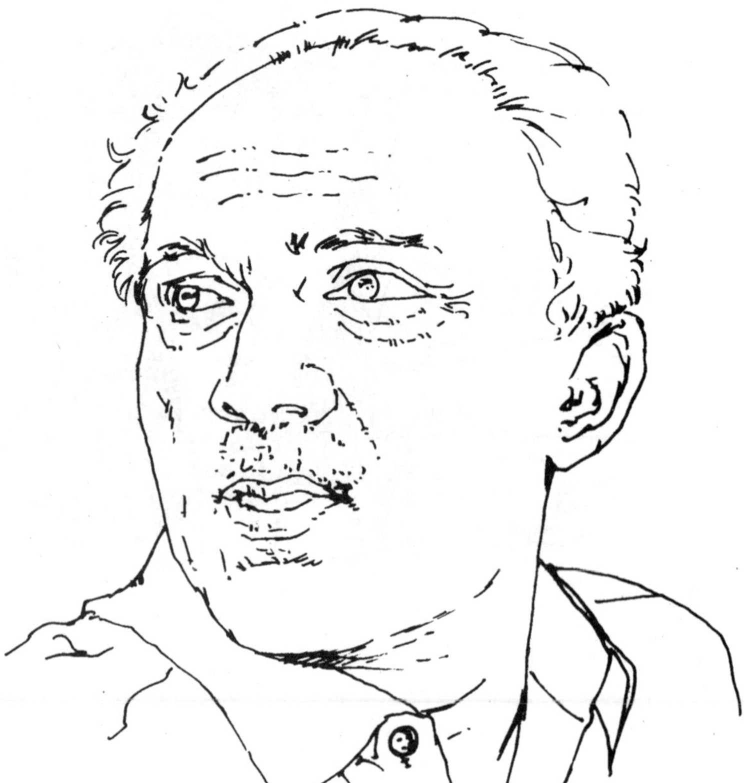

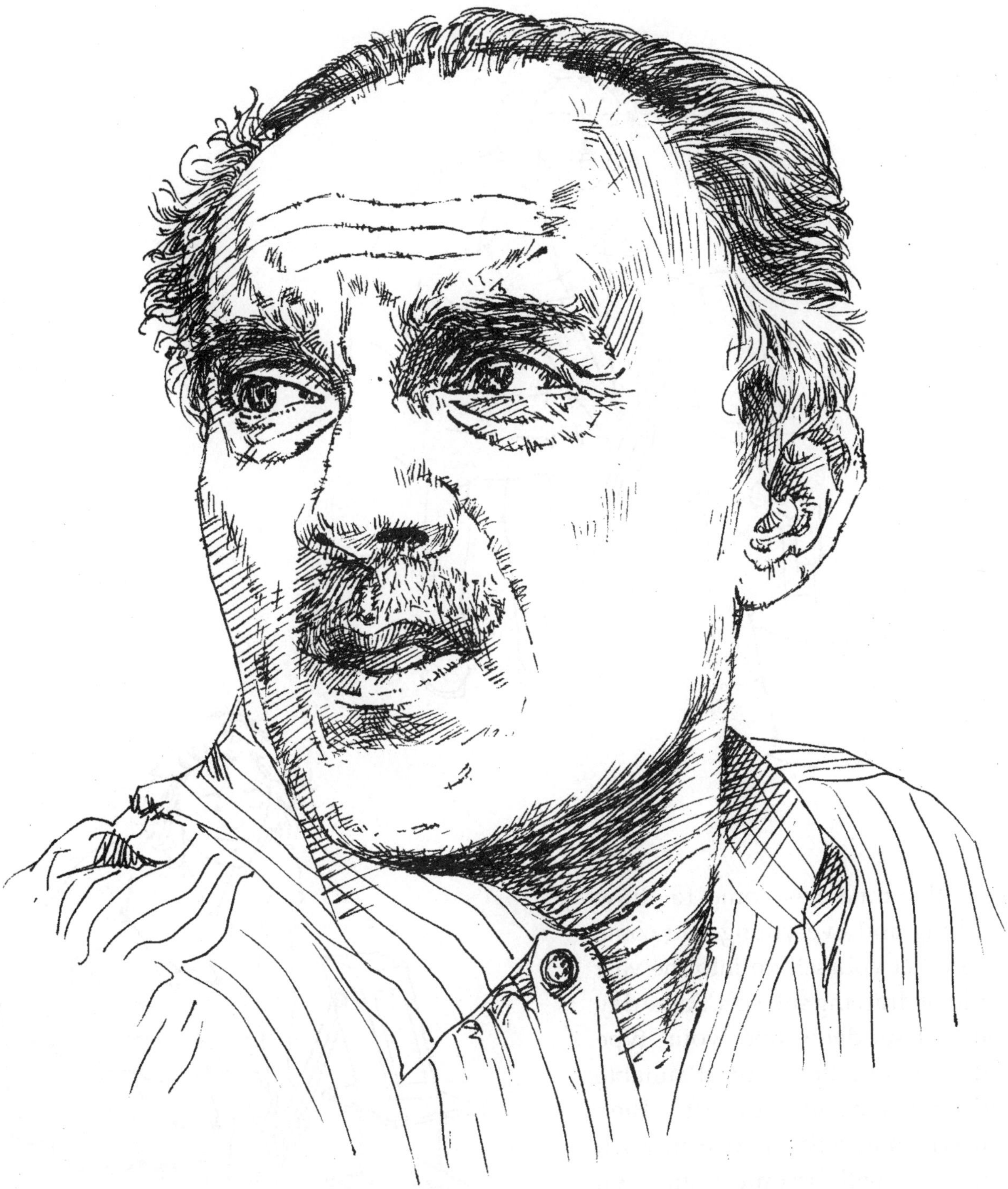

An intellectual and a newspaperman. Does he seem to look like an editor? Correct drawing of facial features brings out the real character of the person.

Let's Go

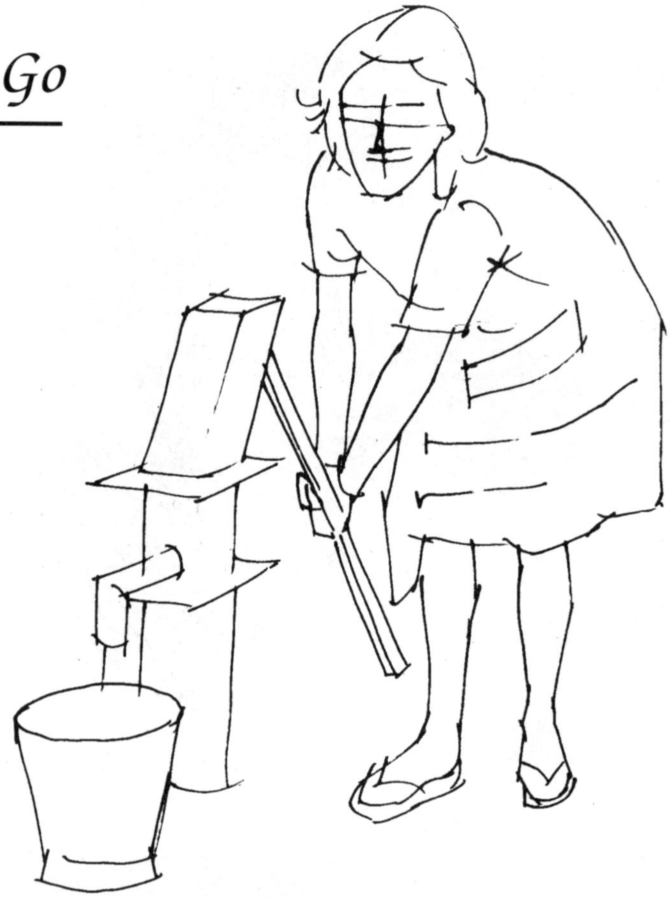

Now the time has come to draw anything and everything you come across. Let yourself go into the vast world of drawing subjects. Some day you will suddenly find 'your' type and style, one that is most suitable and interesting to your taste. Then you will not need anyone to push you. You will become your own guide, master and student, all rolled into one.

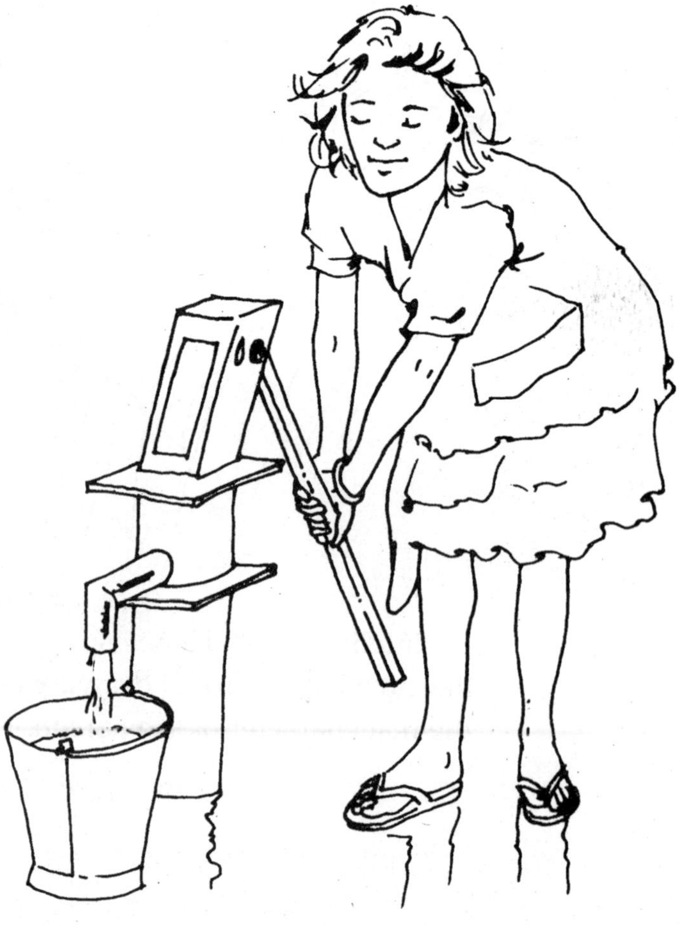

Reflections and water bubbles are important in this drawing. When combined with some other things, the human figure appears more graceful.

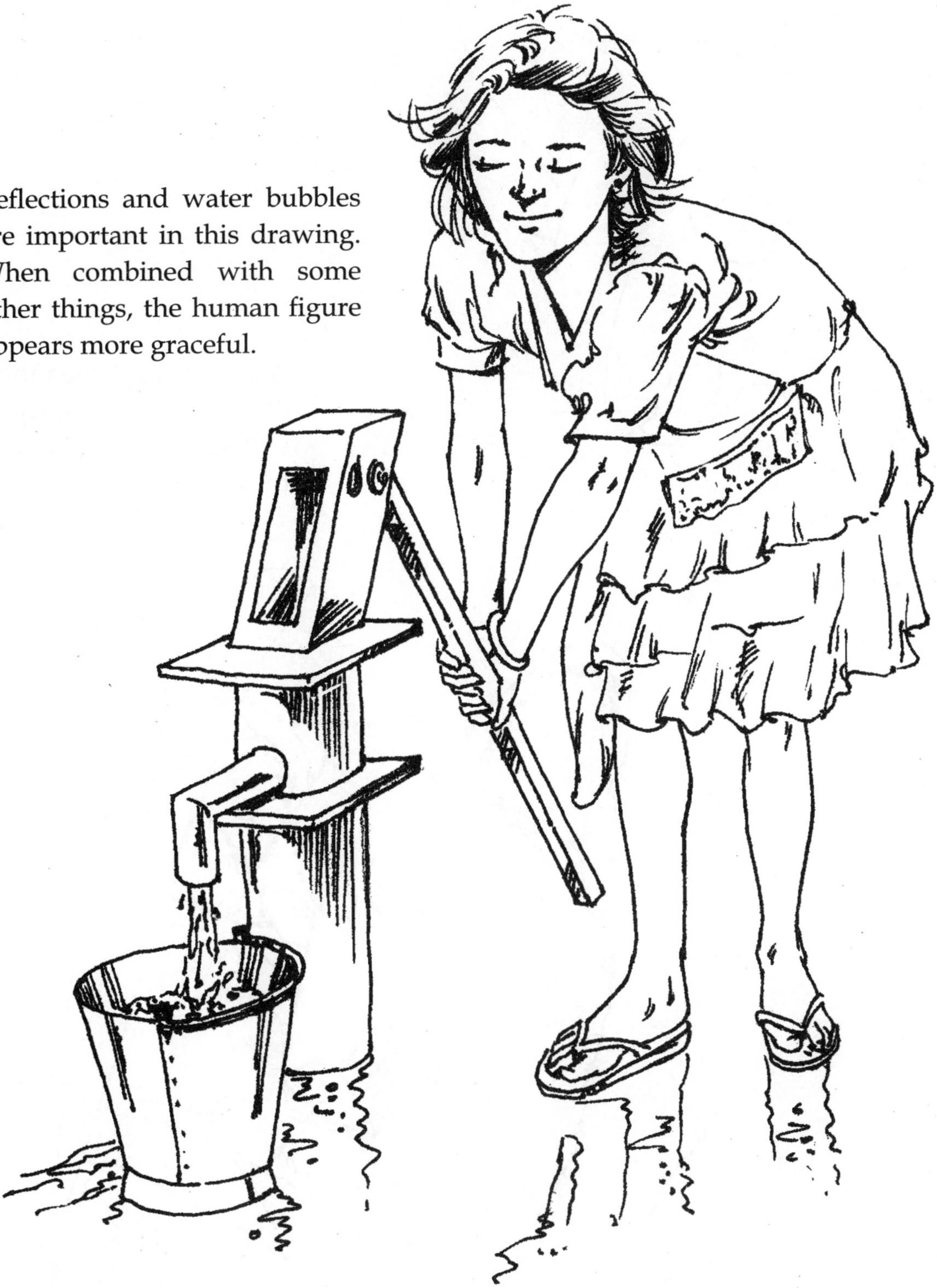

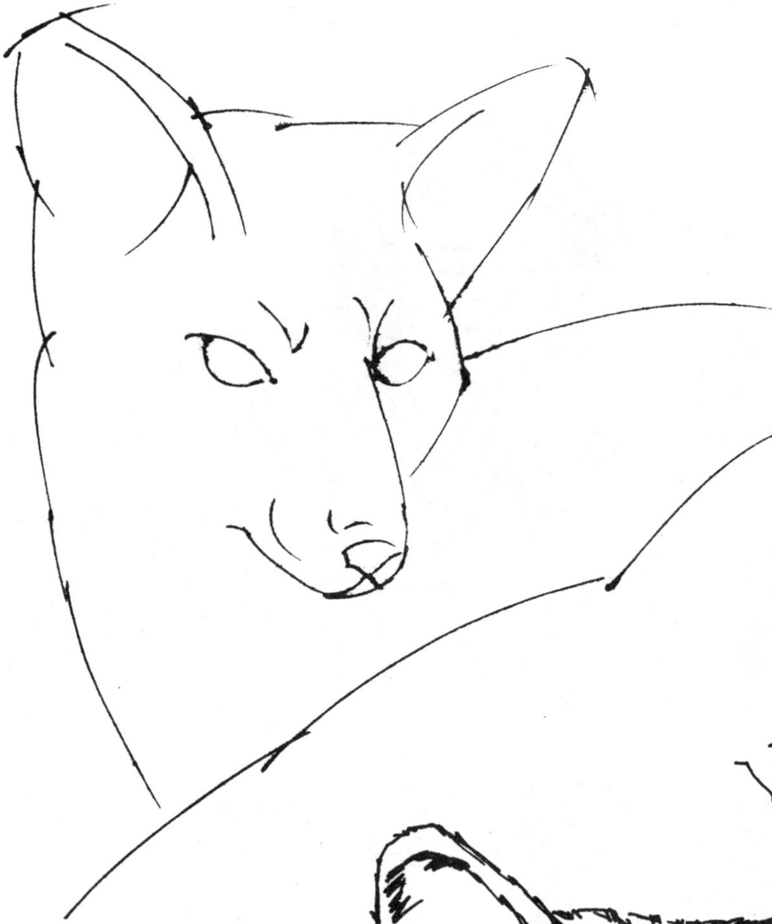

A fox is a suspicious animal. One or two grass saplings will keep it hidden behind the rocky earth.

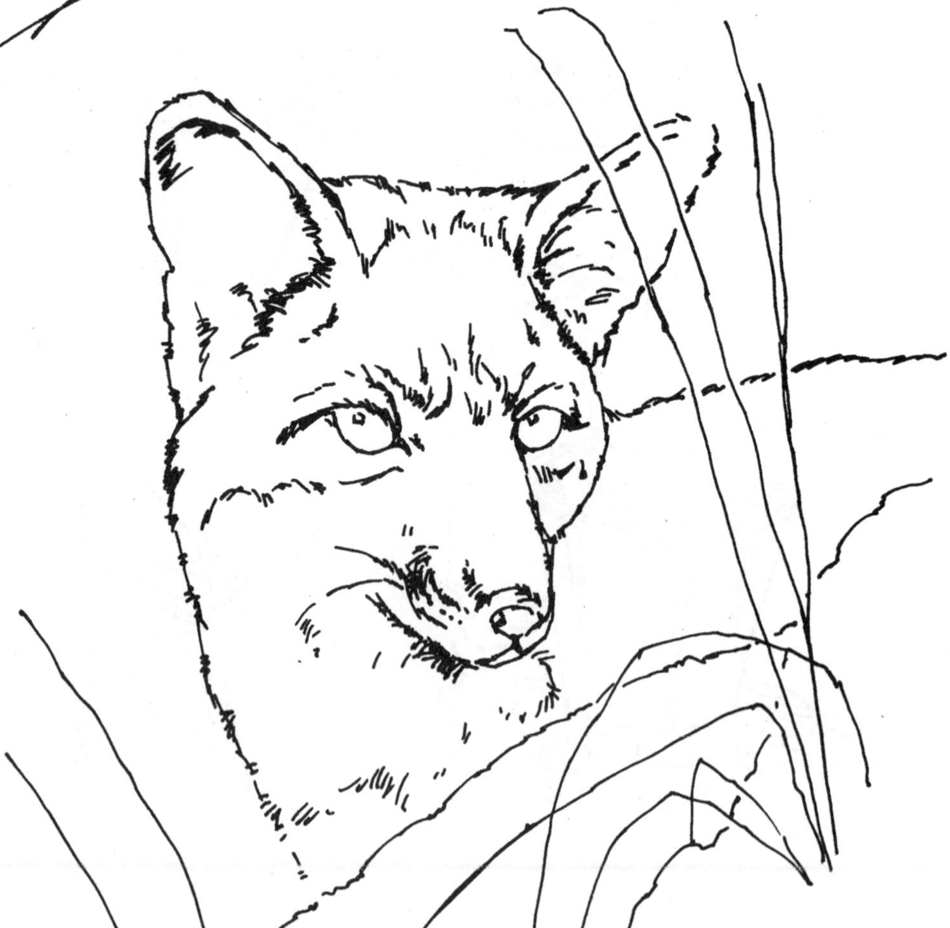

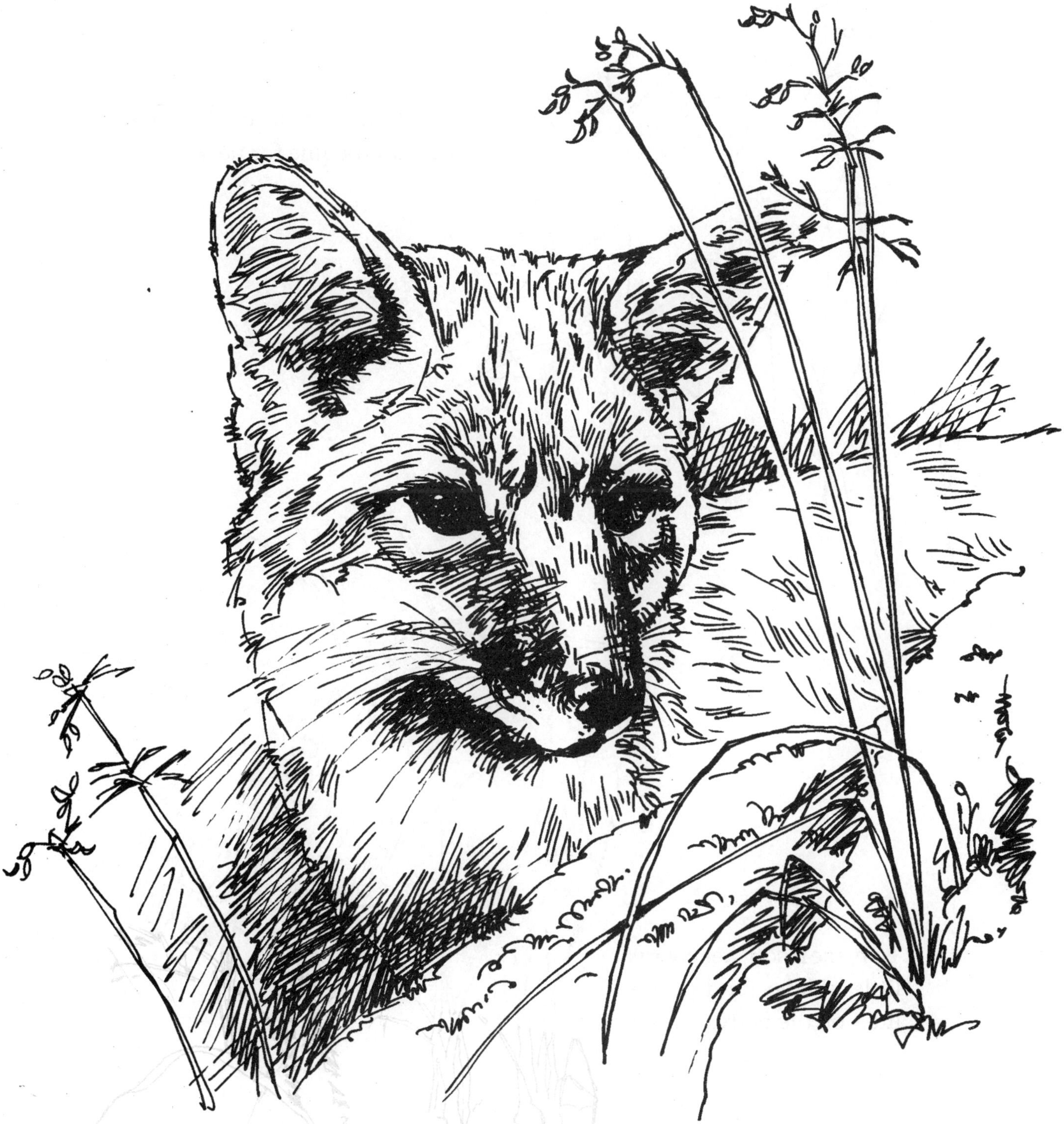

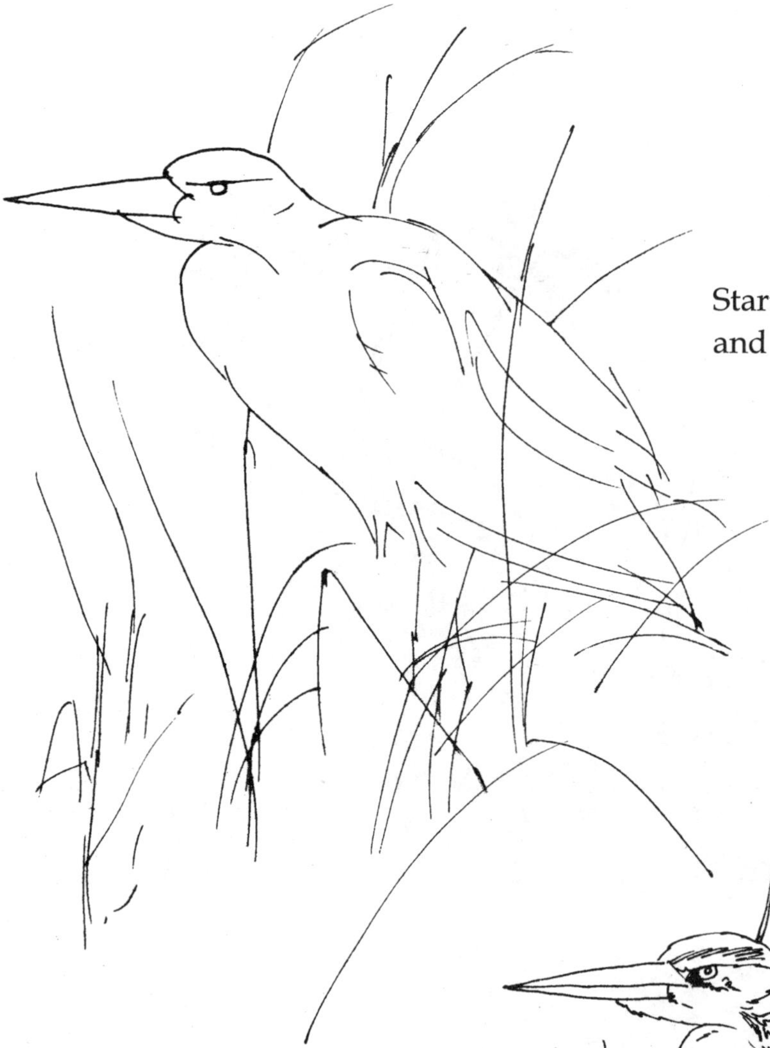

Start with simple oval shape and add the line for neck.

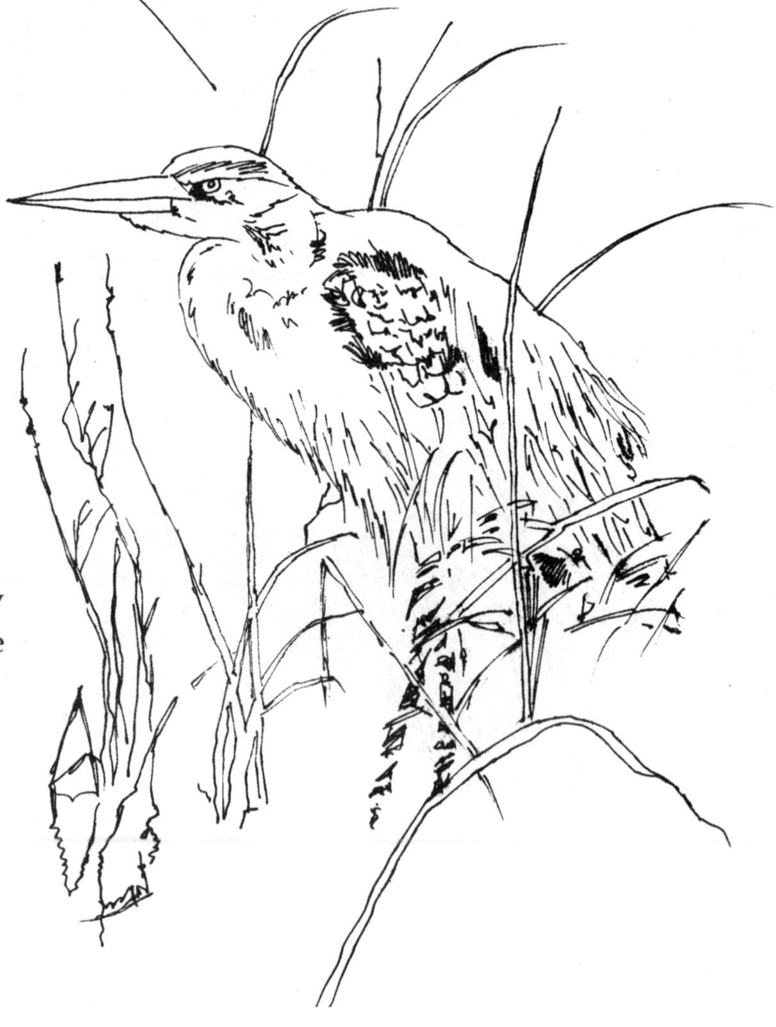

To make it soft, keep very little shades and more lines on the body.

Placing it in the water makes it more natural and at home.

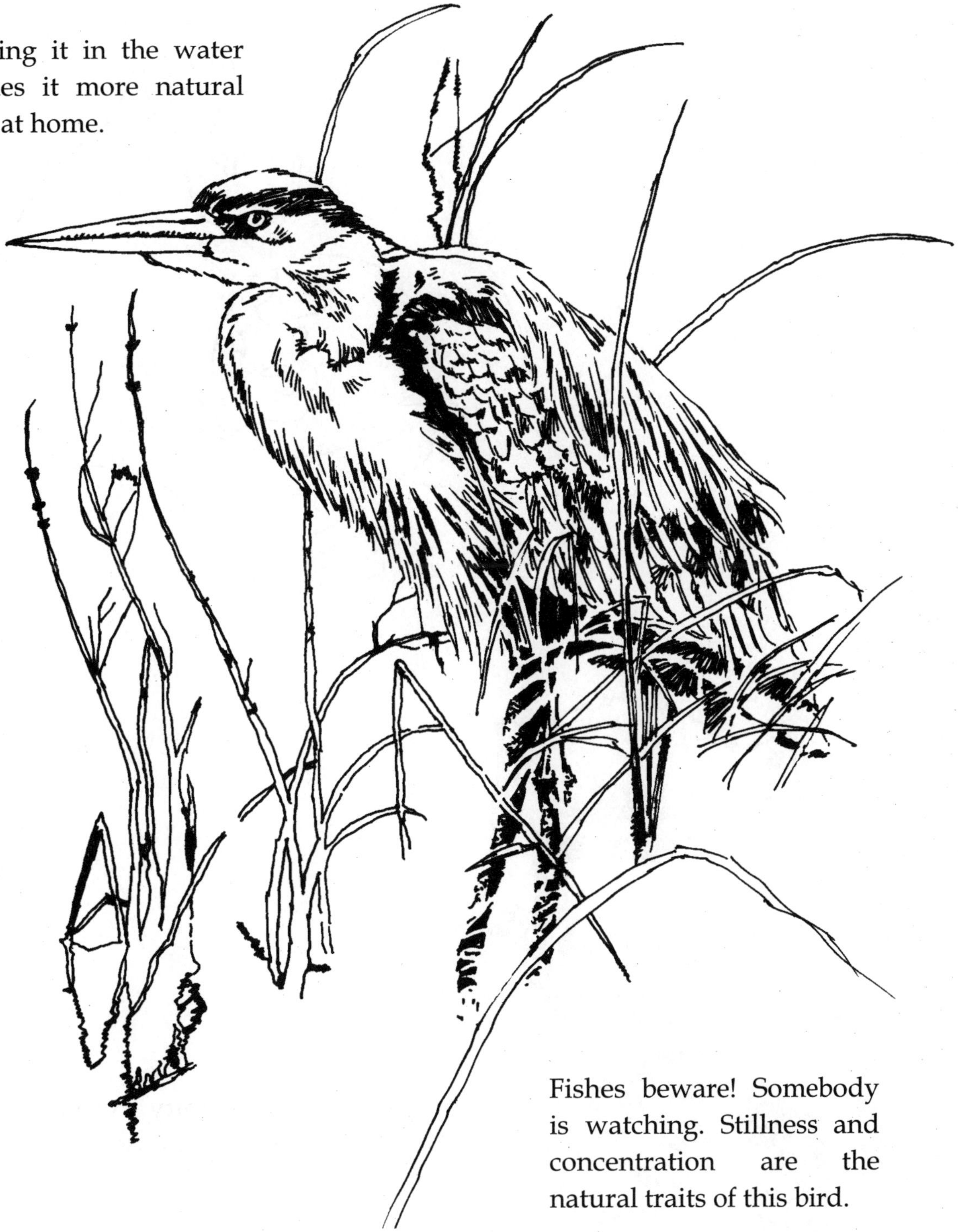

Fishes beware! Somebody is watching. Stillness and concentration are the natural traits of this bird.

Mind that size of the ears and the shape of lips.

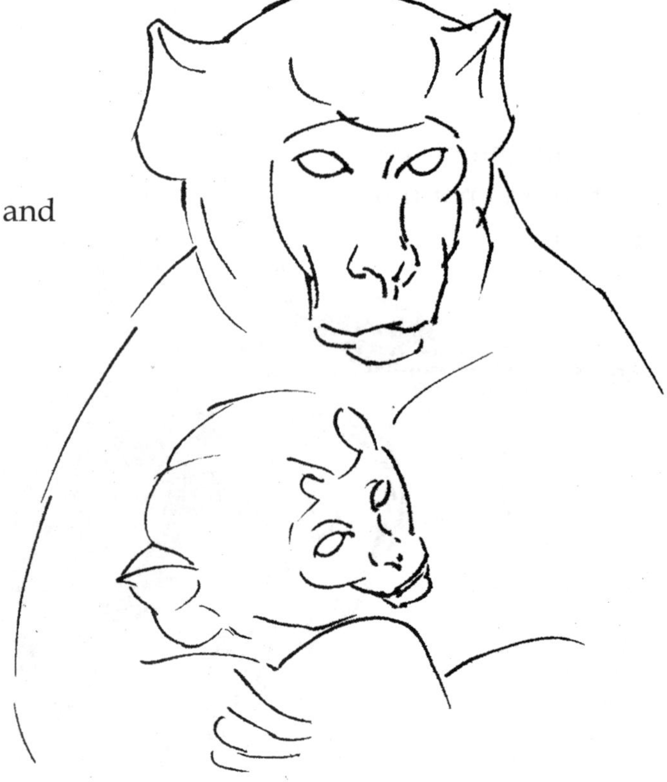

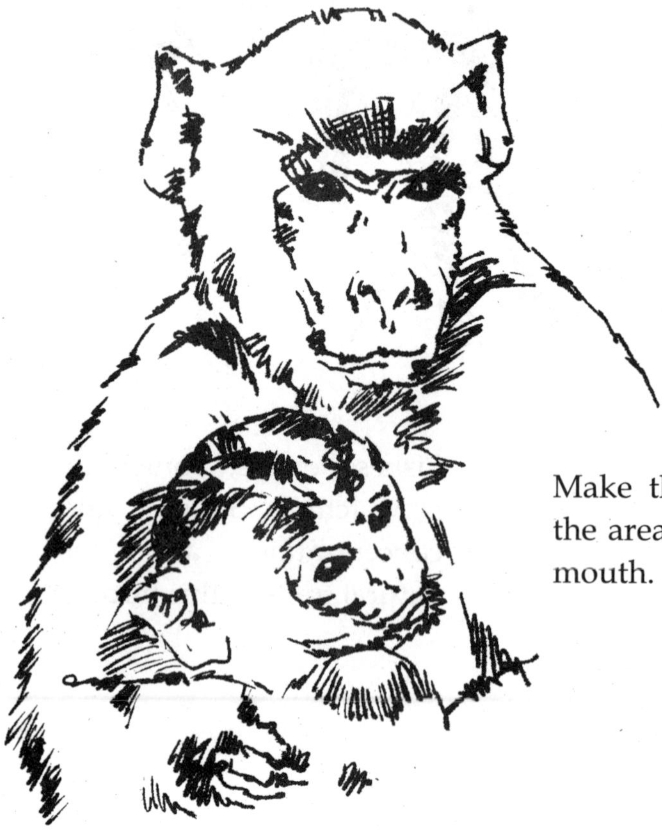

Make them really hairy except the areas around eyes, nose and mouth.

Monkeys are a curious and naughty lot. They like to play with things. Due to their destructive nature, they use and destroy whatever they can lay their hands on.

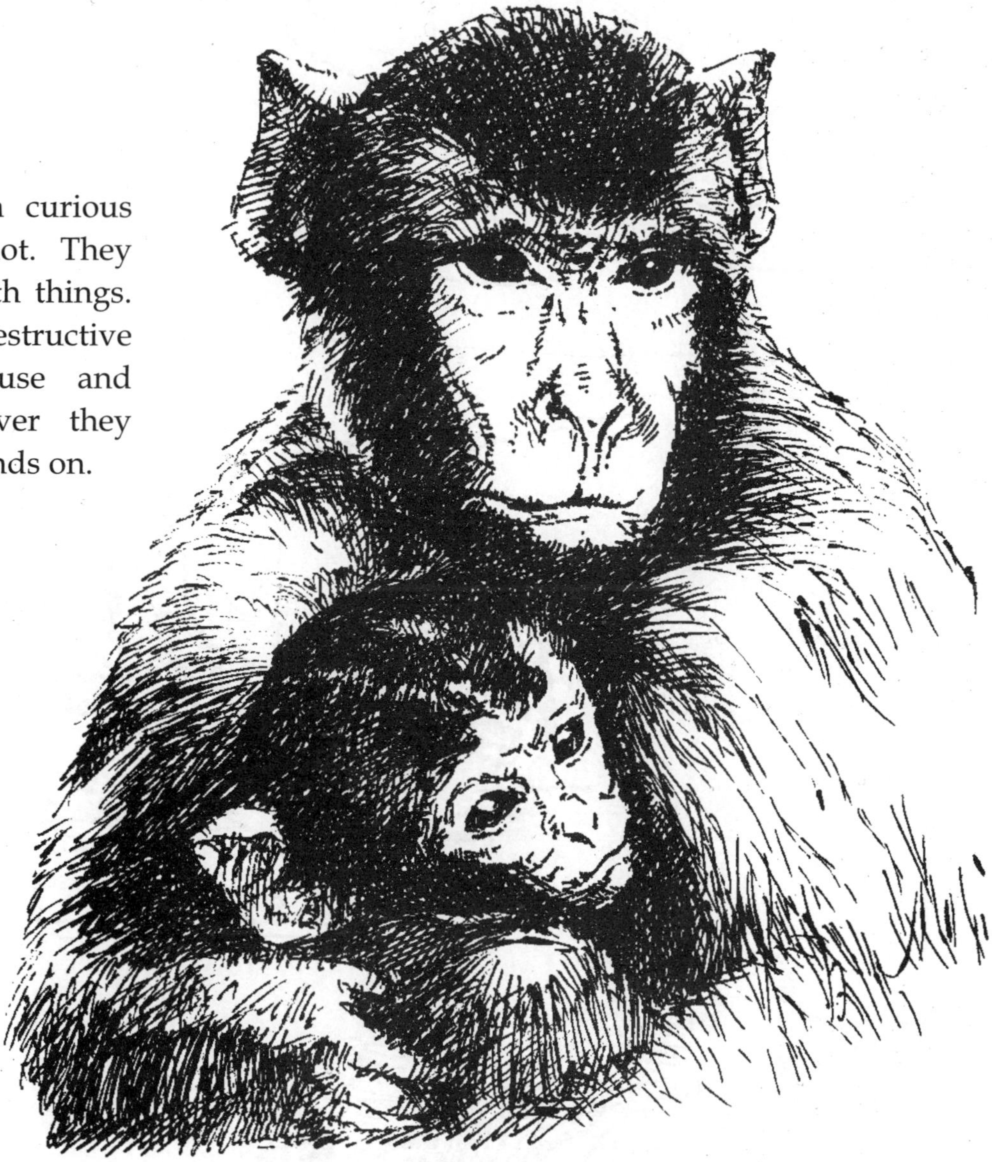

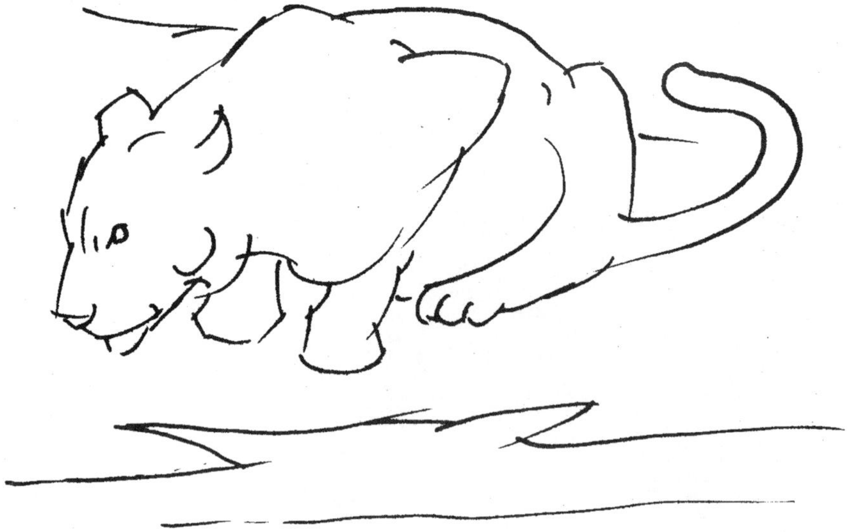

Correct drawing of stripes will do the job for this majestic animal.

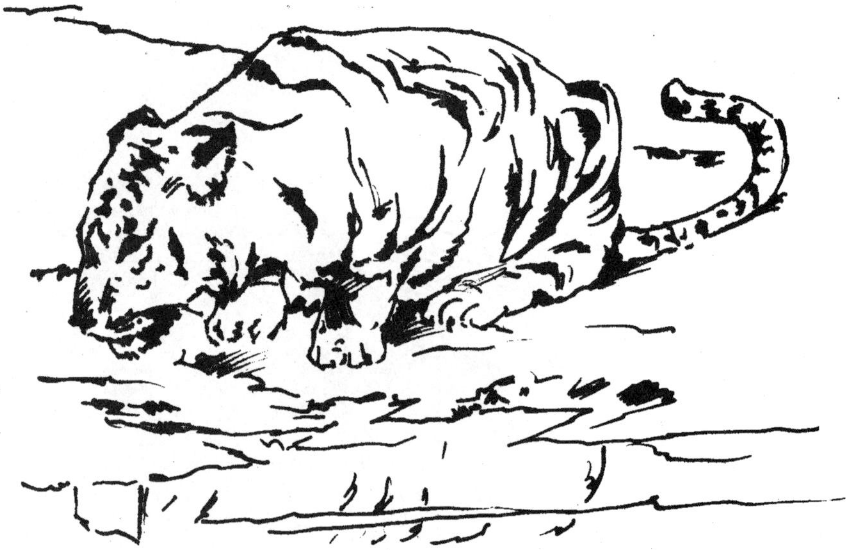

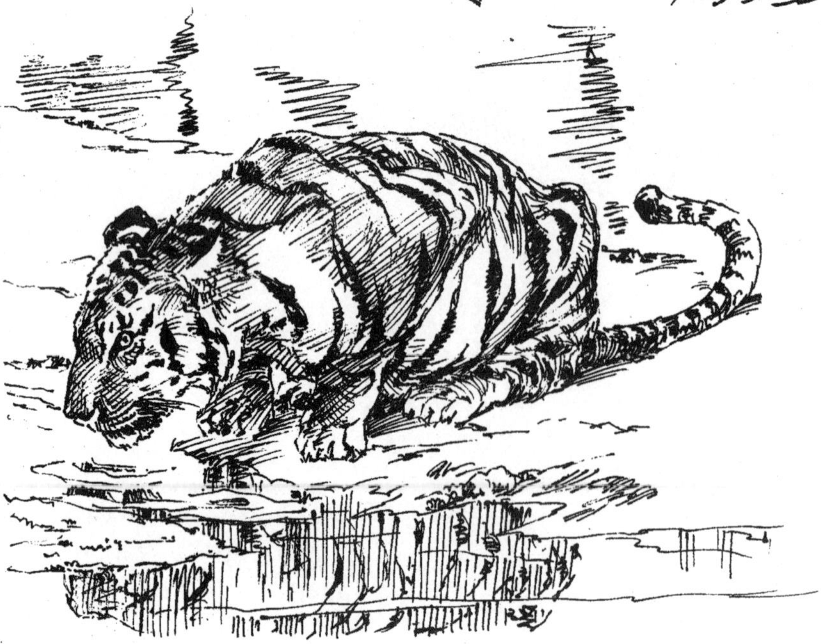

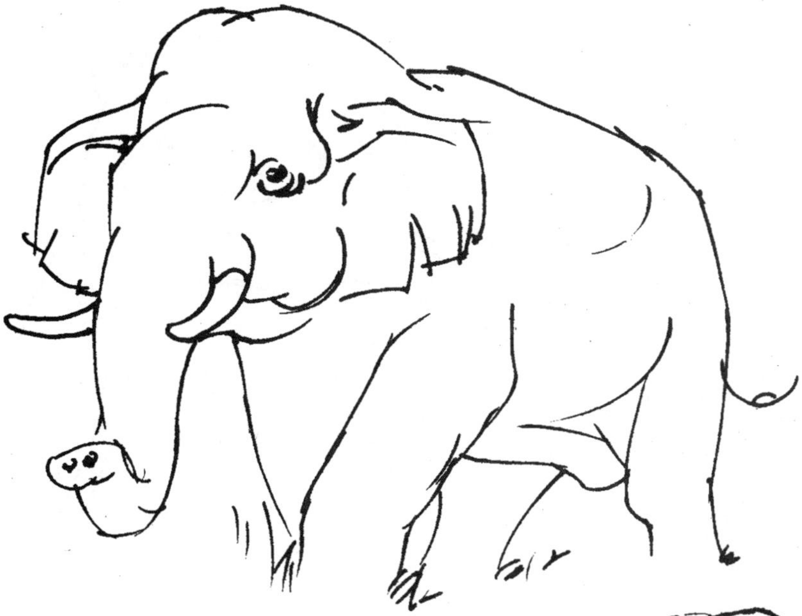

This 'Boss' of the animals really looks heavy. In spite of too many hairy strokes, the smooth outline of the creature keeps its body 'skinny'. Long and round cross-hatch defines the compactness of the body.

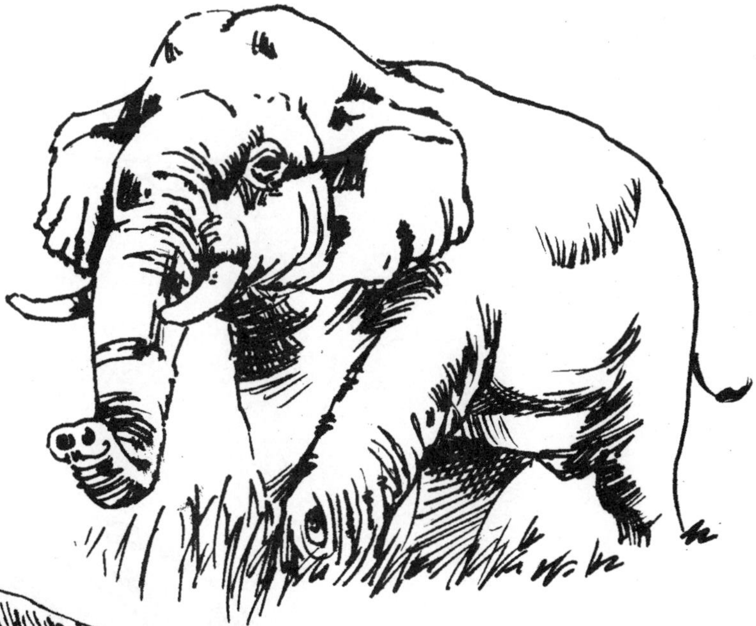

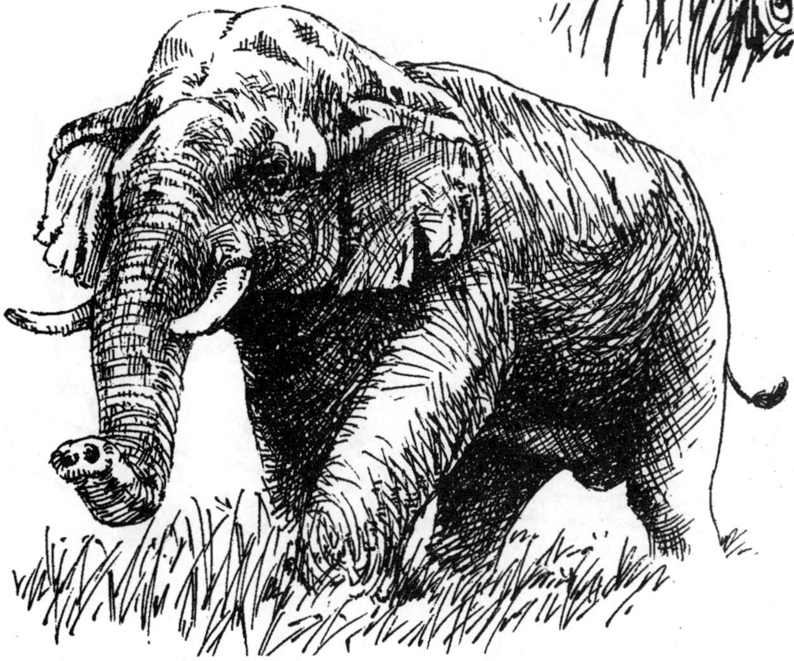

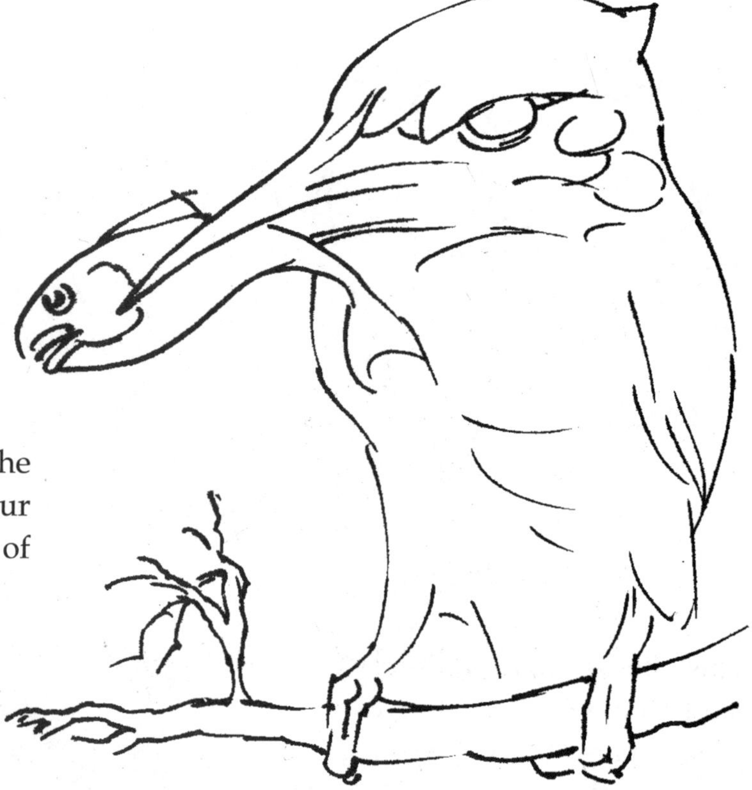

A simple approach to the drawing will lessen your struggle. Finish the head of the bird first.

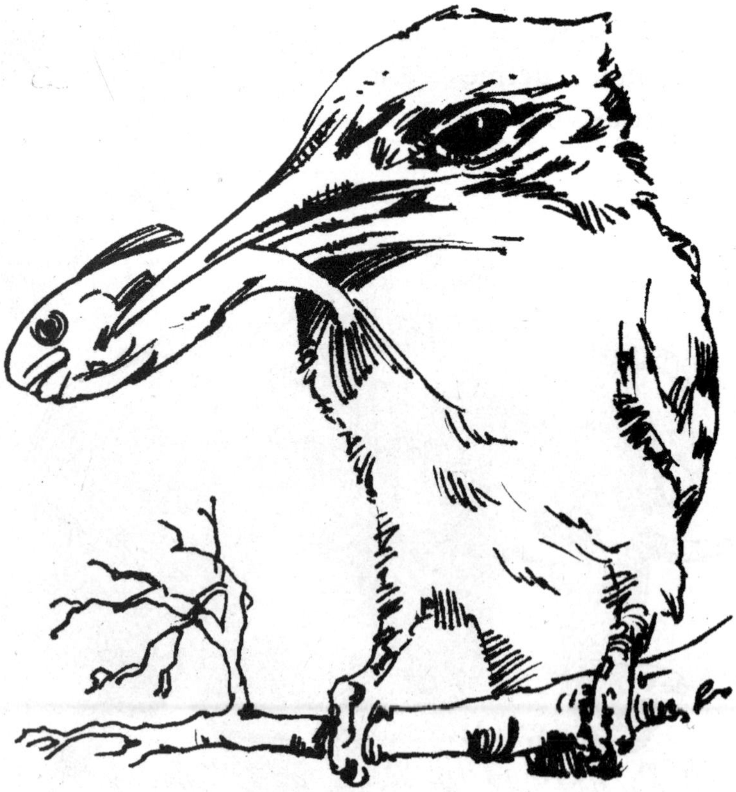

It is challenging to create the difference between fish, bird and the branch.

Another hunter of the fishes. It sits on the branches of trees at the riverside and dives straight into the water to bring out the unfortunate fish.

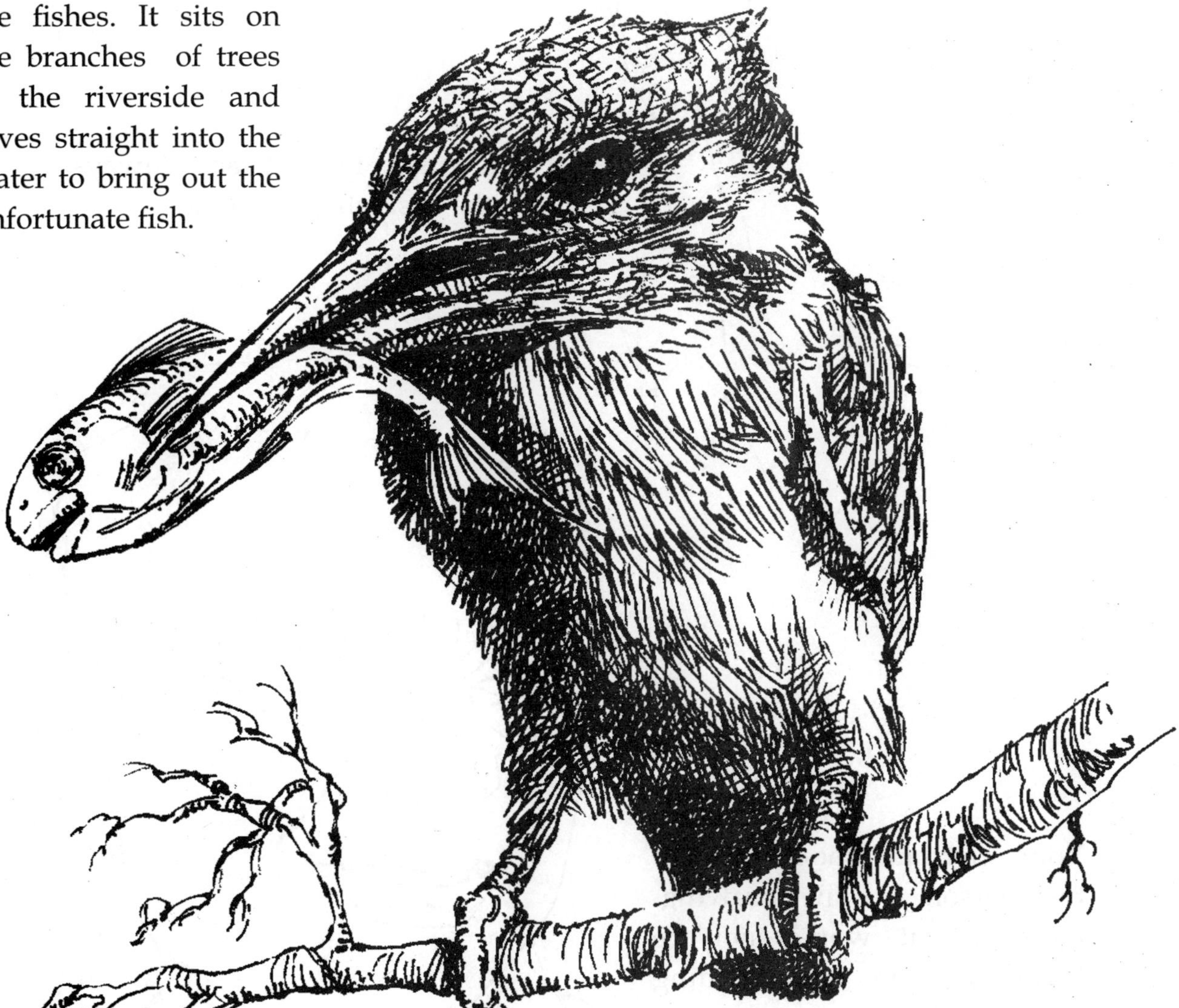

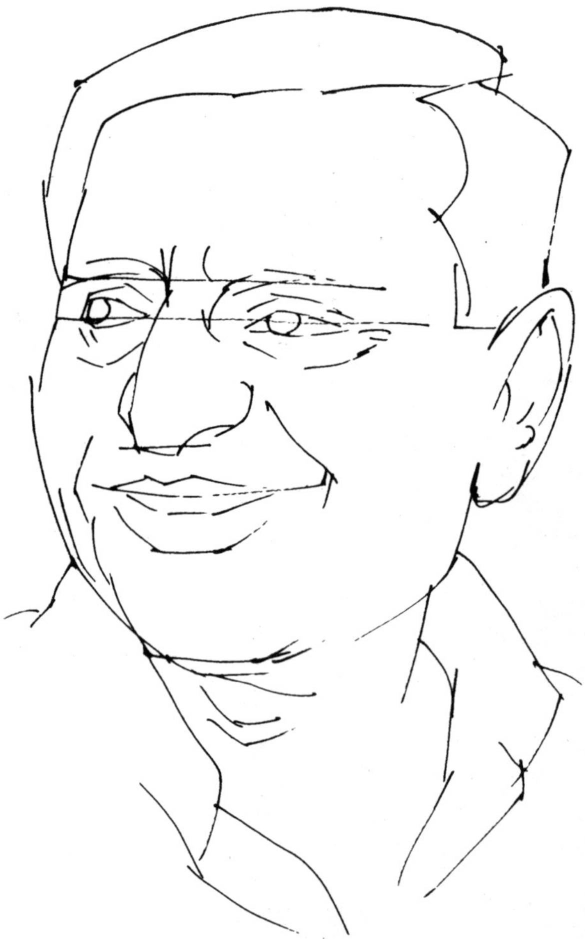

It is a square type of face. Always keep the basic shape in mind.

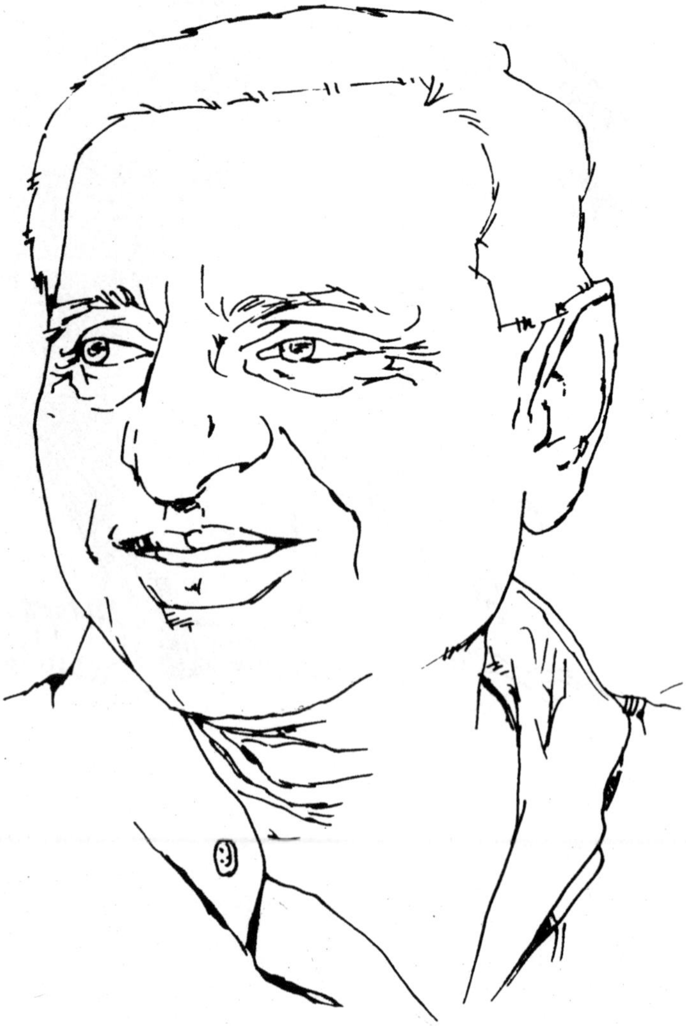

Your portrait should match the person in line drawing. Otherwise it would not be identical even after adding shades and details.

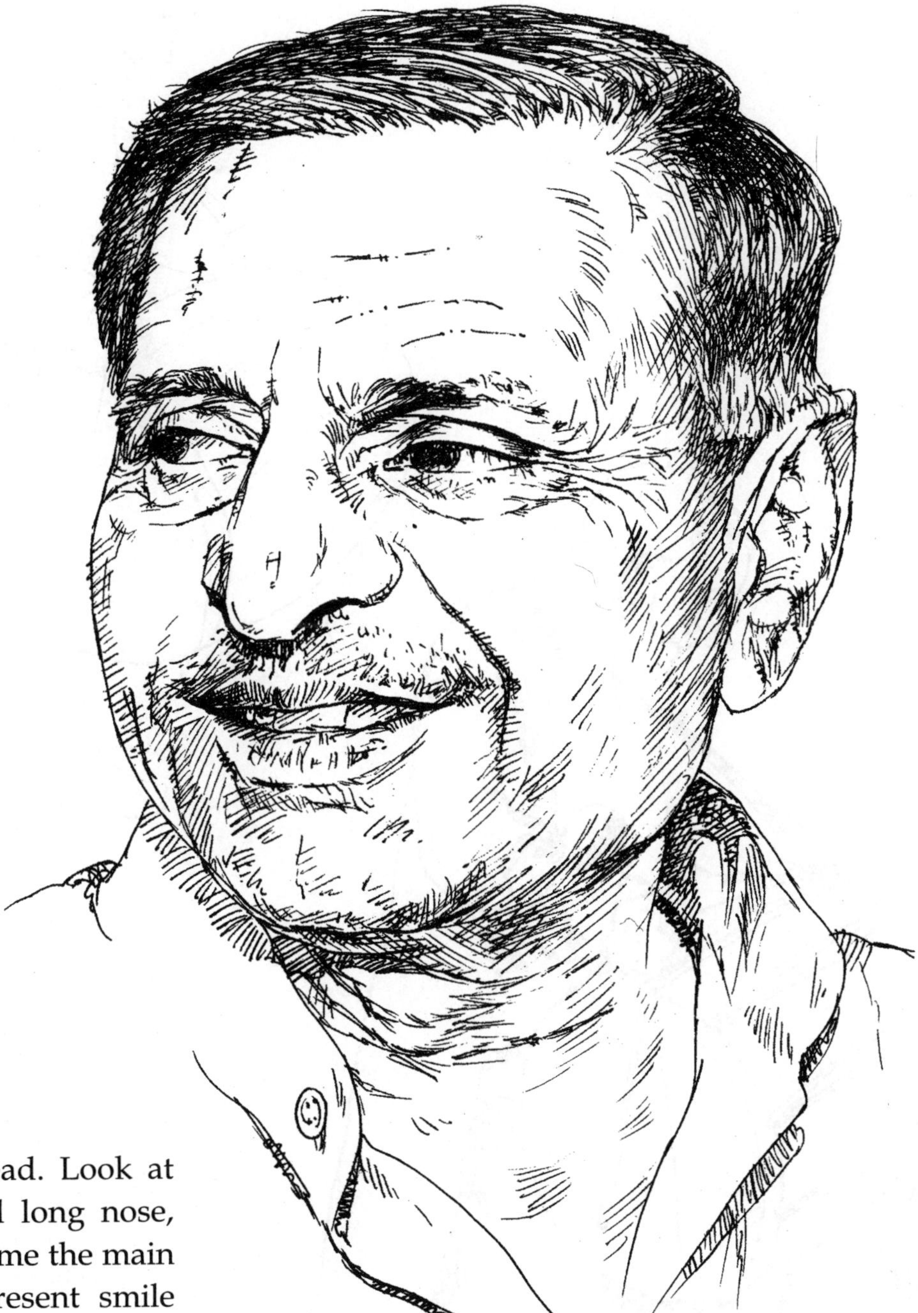

A politician's head. Look at the big ears and long nose, which have become the main features. Ever-present smile of a professional politician is also there.

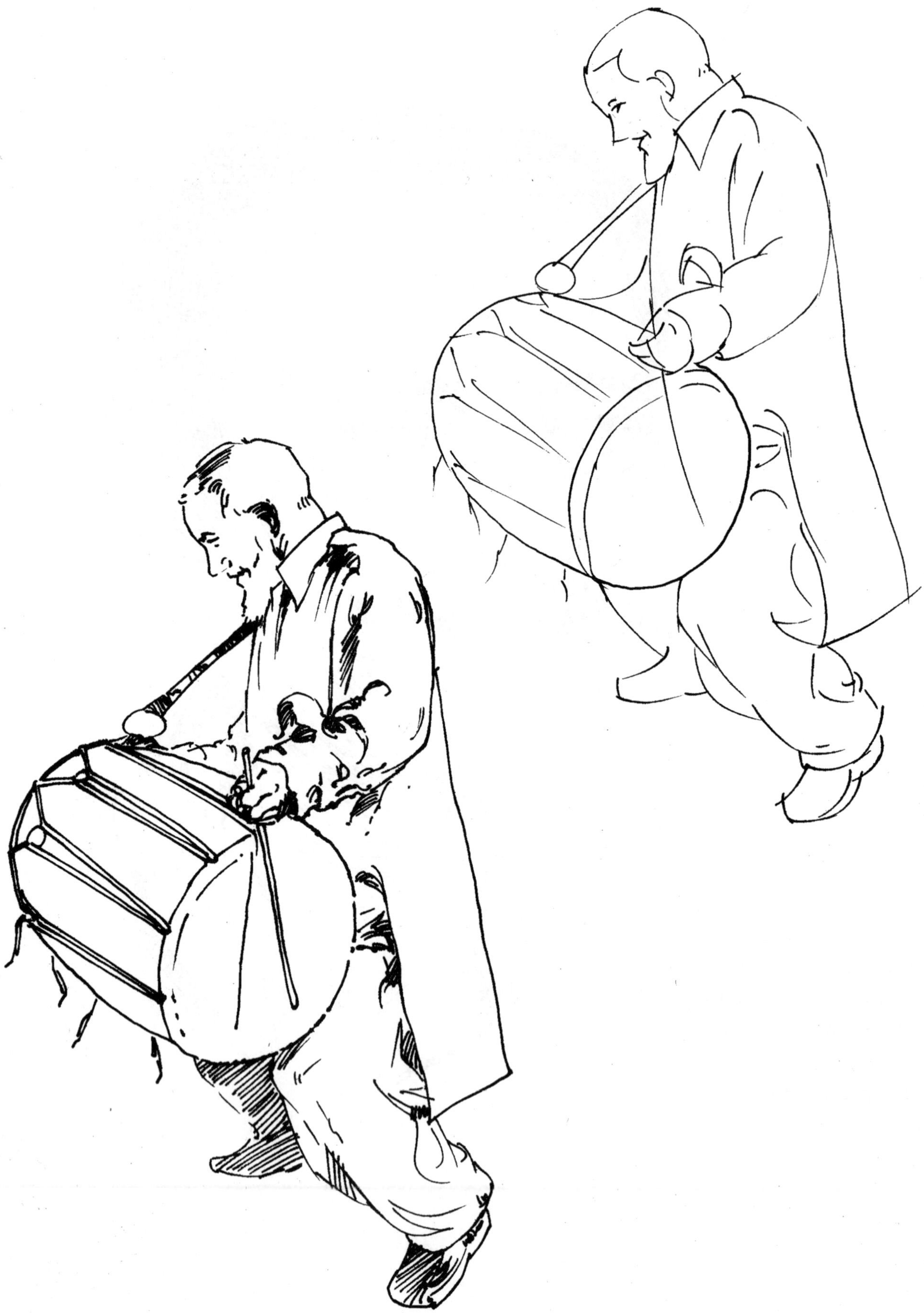

The Dhol and Dholwalas are an integral part of our social life. It may be an occasion like marriage, or a festival like Holi, Dholwalas are always in demand. You have to make it appear more realistic.

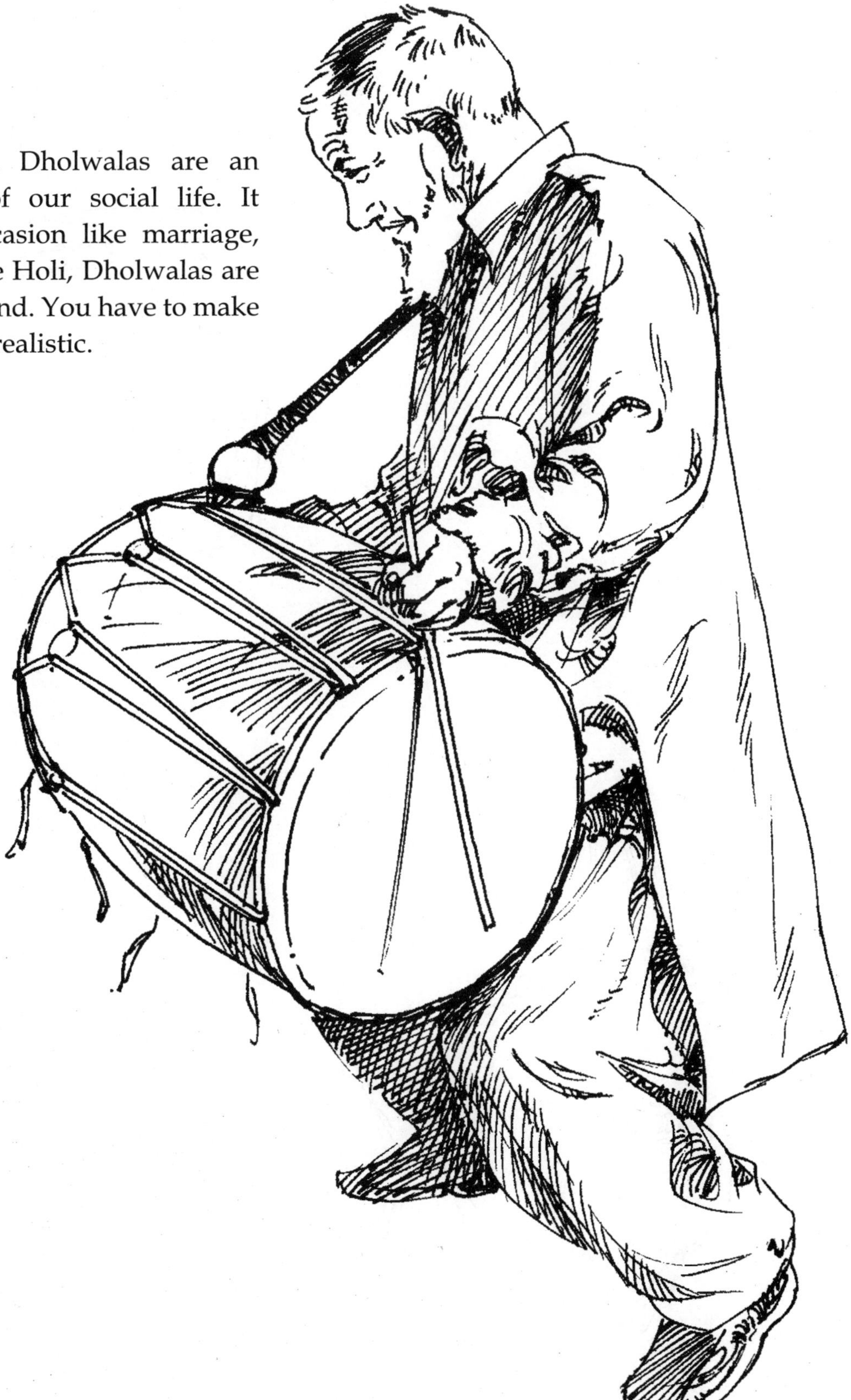

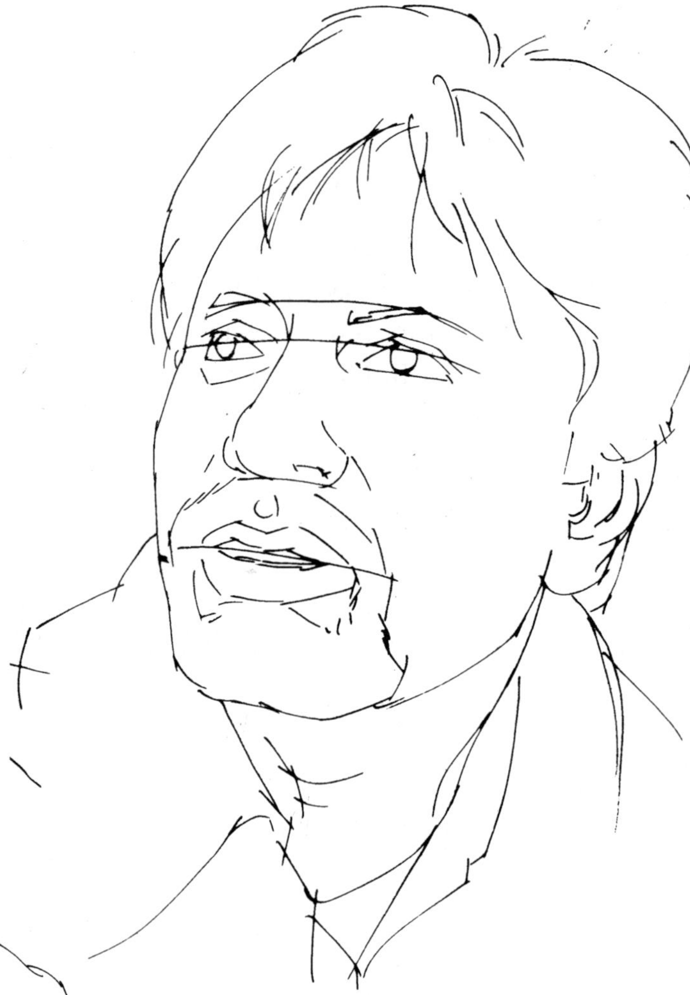

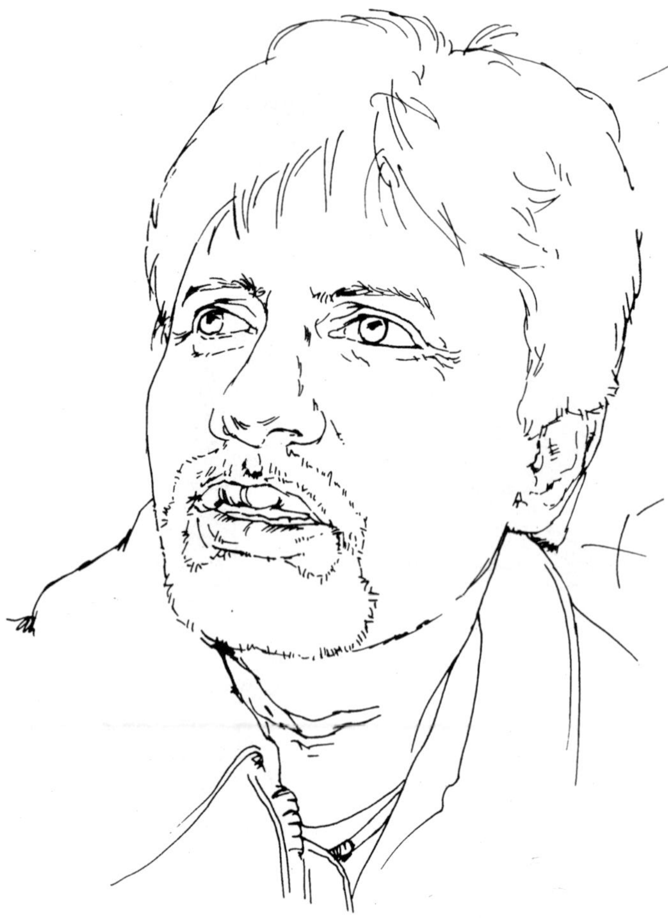

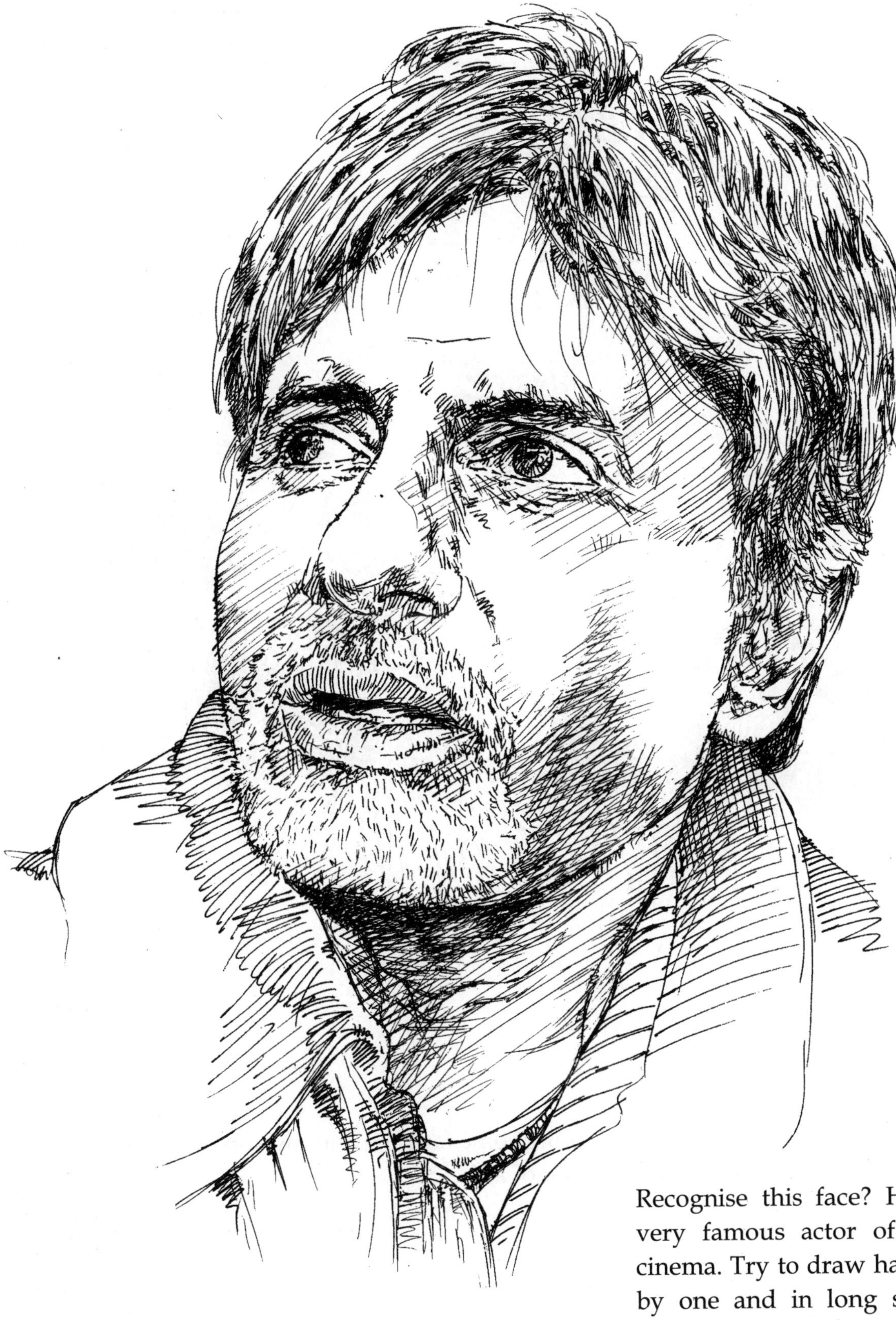

Recognise this face? He is a very famous actor of Hindi cinema. Try to draw hairs one by one and in long strokes. You will be amazed to find the softness you have created.

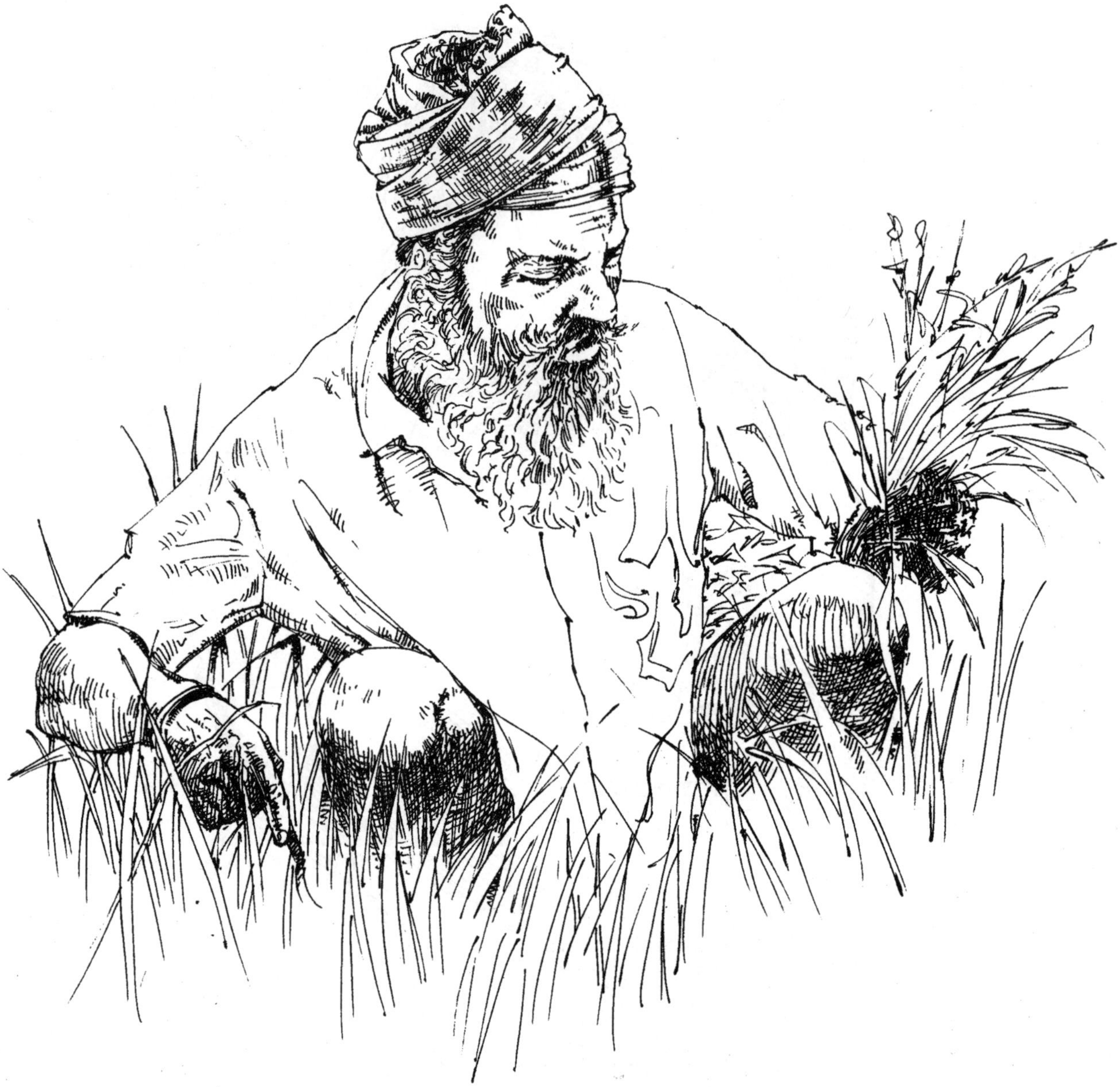

All you need is a 'Sardarji' doing some farming and distance of a few feet. Well, it might be a jackpot of a sketch.

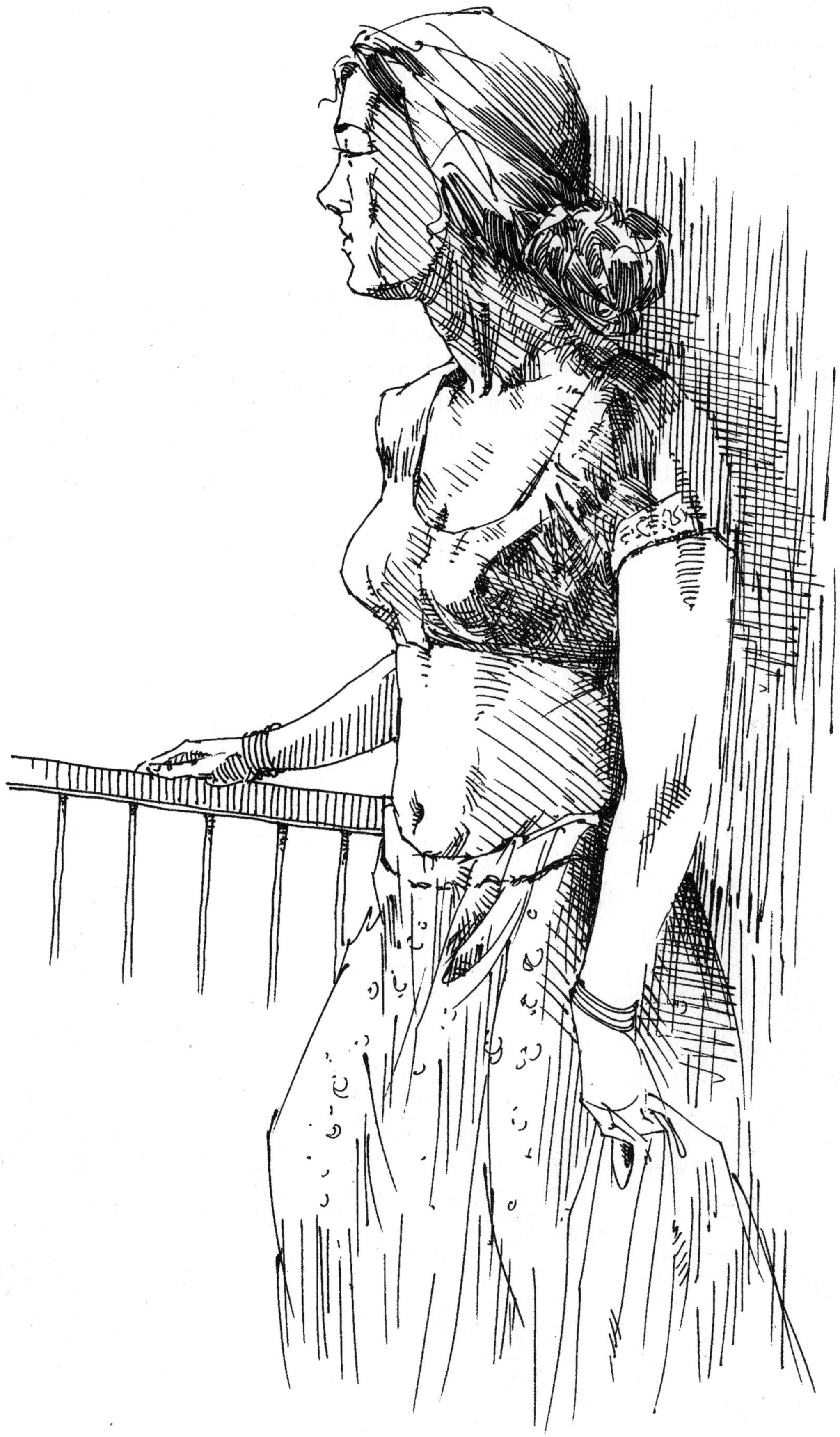

A Few Words

So, friends here we are... at the point where we will part ways. It is been good to be with you all along.

It is time you should start your own journey of exploring and sorting out ways that are more suitable to you. Once you get addicted to it, real fun will enter your life. Pick a pencil and start drawing anything and everything you come across. Draw the rivers, mountains, faces, roads, people, birds, animals... the list is endless. And so is the journey of drawing. Once you reach a destination, you will try to seek out new ones. I hope and wish that this book has been of some help to you. Remember, painting is living, so enjoy every line and shape you draw. This attitude will keep you going. Happy journey...

Ajay

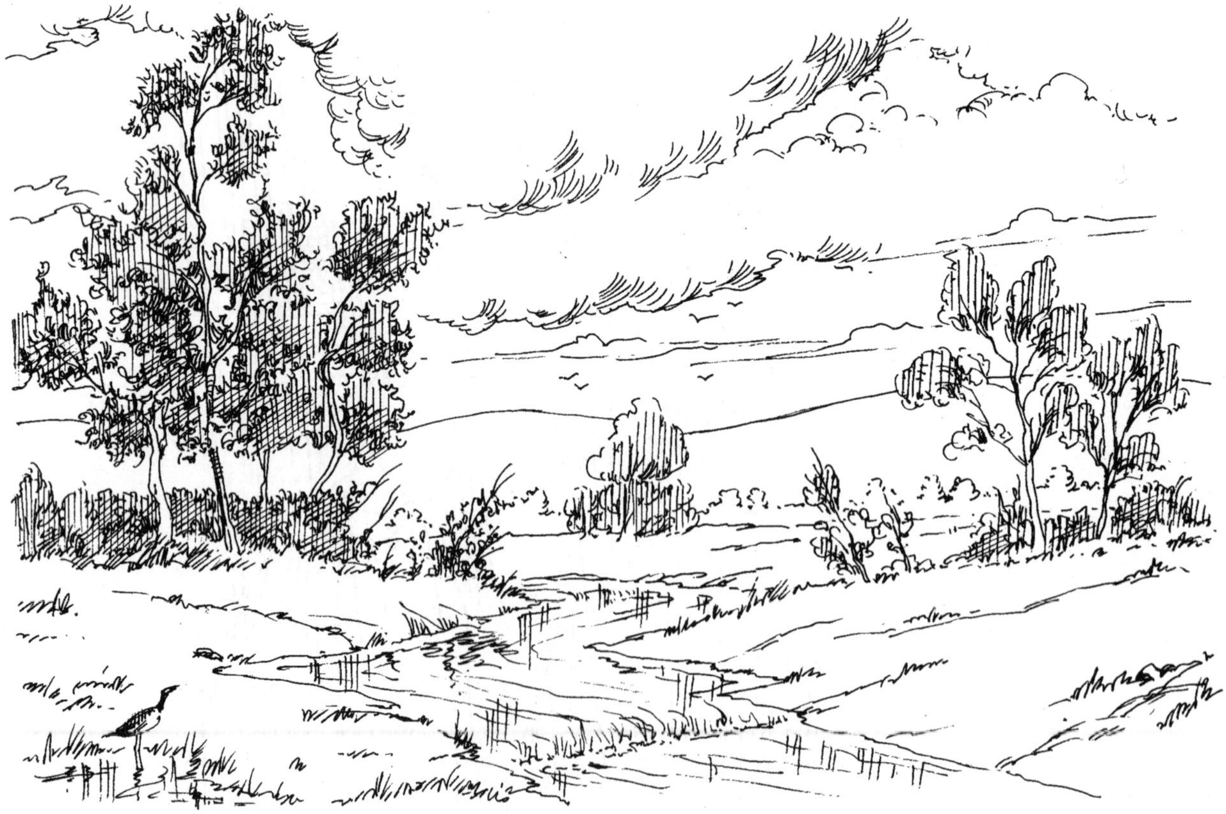